MW01288474

THIS BOOK IS A THREE PART COLLECTION THAT OFFERS MY READERS THE ENTIRE STORY THAT WAS PUBLISHED UNDER THE "YOU ARE WORTHY TOO" MINISTRY IN 2014.

IT IS MY HOPE THAT BY PUTTING ALL THREE OF THESE BOOKS INTO ONE THAT MORE PEOPLE WILL HAVE THE OPPORTUNITY TO READ WHAT GOD CALLED ME FORTH TO SHARE.

WHILE I CERTAINLY AM NOT PROUD OF ALL I HAVE DONE IN MY LIFETIME, I AM PROUD TO BE A SERVANT OF THE MOST HIGH GOD.

I TRULY BELIEVE NO MATTER WHERE YOU ARE AT WITH YOUR WALK WITH GOD, THIS FULL 3 PART SEQUEAL WILL INCREASE YOUR FAITH.

IT WILL UNDOUBTEDLY MAKE YOU LAUGH AND CRY AND LAUGH AGAIN! AFTER ALL, ISN'T THAT WHY WE READ BOOKS TO BEGIN WITH!

ISBN 9781505696431

90000 >

9 781505 696431

You Are Worthy Too

The Proof is in the Pudding:

The complete first 3 volumes of my true life story

By Wendy Glidden

Copyright 2014 Wendy Glidden

Table of Contents

Dear Reader,

First I want to take this opportunity to thank you for purchasing my book! This is the complete collection of all the true life stories that I previously published in 2014.

This book takes you from the beginning of my story, through my first 22 years of life and ends with 12 true life stories that have taken place over the course of my last 20 years! I have also included two bonus chapters from upcoming titles!

I am thrilled to be able to offer this collection at a reduced cost by putting all three volumes into one book! It is always my prayer to be a light in the darkness. To be a sister in Christ that seeks to help others find their way back onto the narrow path. While many think of the narrow path as 'no fun', I am here to assure you that is not the case! Life begins once you discover the truth!

It is my hope that in reading all the true life events that God called me forth to share that you find your faith strengthened. I would love nothing more than to hear from you! Of course I would also love for you to share my story with anyone you think may benefit!

With each purchase, I find myself one step closer to witnessing the fulfillment of my childhood dreams. Please help me spread the message that God gave me in 2012:

"You Are Worthy Too!"

Wendy Glidden

You Are Worthy Too

In The Beginning

By Wendy Glidden

Copyright 2014 Wendy Glidden

Dear Reader,

First I want to take this opportunity to thank you for purchasing my book! This is the beginning of my story. The first full sixteen years of them are in this volume!

All my life I dreamt of being a writer. I wanted my books to fill people with hope. As I grew up, I continued to write off and on but I had long given up on ever publishing anything to encourage others or brighten their days.

As I approached my 40s, I began questioning life and relationships. Then a life event of my own caused me to fall to my knees. I had finally come to the end of my own strength and determination. It was in giving everything to God, He gave me the desires of my heart.

I truly hope you enjoy this first book full of true chapters from my life.

When God convicted me, He showed me how He had been there all along. You get some insights as you are shown things through the rearview mirror!

There is much the Lord is leading me to share. I hope you stick around as I continue to share my life story as well as other titles. Look for all the details on the You Are Worthy Too Website! The link to take you there is on my Connect with Me page at the end of the book.

Had someone asked me a year ago if I thought my life was worthy of publishing I would have laughed and quickly said, "No".

God thought otherwise. He called me out to share my story over a year ago. While full of fear, I stepped out in Faith.

I pray my story leaves you inspired, encouraged and full of faith. I am humbled by your purchase. Be blessed and be a blessing!

Love, Wendy Glidden

Chapter One

In the beginning

My name is Wendy Glidden. I have been pregnant 13 times in my life! Ten of those babies, I have personally raised myself. One of them I gave up for adoption. The one prior to her and the one after her, I chose not to have at all. That decision, along with a few more, allowed me to believe that I was not worthy of God's love.

My life has been eventful to say the least and God has called me to become what He told me I would be as a child; A mom of many.

A mom, I have come to learn is simply someone who nurtures. Not necessarily someone who gives birth to a human being.

While it is true I have given birth to many children, we must remember God is humorous and in giving me all of these children, well, He has taught me to be humorous myself!

I really am unsure of how to start this book and how to proceed with the ministry He has put in my heart and I am relying on the Holy Spirit to lead me.

I have always believed in honesty, yet I have lived hiding my biggest sins in the closet. I make you this promise my friend; by doing that I allowed the evil one to keep me from my work.

It was just this year that I captured the negative thoughts that the evil one has been whispering to me daily. Among them were phrases such as:

I am not worthy

I am not qualified to lead

Who would listen to me?

I am a joke

I am a murderer

Now I have been growing for the last few years spiritually by leaps and bounds. Even with God calling me so loudly to do His work, in my head this is what I was subconsciously hearing. That is NOT what God has to say about His children!

I am a child of God. I was told so 30 years ago by an angel. Even with that, I allowed the evil one to get in my way and even worse for me, to remain there!

It is my hope that with me allowing the Holy Spirit to work through me that I can help countless others avoid the trials and tribulations I have gone through myself, or at least help them out of the pit of hell quicker than I made my own great escape!

I had to make this leap of faith today and begin sharing my story when I had no idea what I would say! This is my opening page. Sharing my story with any who decide to read it.

Remember our God is stronger, our God is Mighty. Through Him All things are possible.

May you have a blessed day,

Wendy, Mom of Many!

Chapter Two

I Will Never! Me and My 'Oh So Righteous Self'

Be careful when you exclaim you will never do something! More than I care to admit, I have found myself doing the exact thing I was so righteously convinced I would never do! After all, I was out to please God and be a great servant for Him. I had big plans. I was a good girl! The list of things I would never do was never ending. Allow me to highlight some of the bigger ones right off the top of my head:

1. Go against God's will for my life

2. Get angry at God

3. Yell at God

4. Spite God

5. Have an abortion

6. Give a baby up for adoption

7. Smoke

8. Drink

9. Do drugs

10. Be one of 'those' girls

11. Stay in an abusive relationship

12. Find myself on the brink of becoming part of the porn

industry

Impressive list don't you think? Oh, you know I have to address each and every one of these because in all honesty, I have done all of them. We all know there are many more lurking out there in the background. I'm sure the evil one will try to taunt me with any that remain!

I'm amazed as I see the ink on the paper. Am I really going to share all of this? I know the answer. Yes. I am. For you see it is all of my sins that I have committed that make it that much more amazing that God has called me to share my story. I pray for guidance and protection as I proceed. It is my focus to show you that all of us ARE WORTHY of God's grace.

I want you to realize I did all these things after receiving the knowledge I received when I was young. While many in the world have never built a relationship with the Lord, I can't make that claim. That truth is just one of many reasons I believed I was no longer worthy of God's love.

Can you for one minute imagine being told you would be a mother to many when your own mother was the saddest darkest most negative person you knew on a daily basis? I wanted nothing to do with her life's path.

I was just a preteen when I was told by God that my first child would be a girl. It was also revealed to me that I would be young when I had her.

I cried for I don't know how long after this was all told to me. I also wrote in my diary what was spoken to me and I began an outline of what kind of parent I would be right then and there. How I wish I had that journal to this day. I long to know what all I wrote down about that experience, but my journal perished in a fire in the 15th year of my life.

Regardless, sin number one was accomplished the year I met my first love. With his help, I was going to outsmart God! I laugh about it now, but trust me when I say; this was a pivotal moment in my life.

It is my belief this was the beginning of my entering the age of consent and my sifting was just about to start!

I must end this chapter here and save it before I lose my nerve.

Be blessed and be a blessing to others!

Wendy, mom of many

Chapter Three

How I Learned About God!

The evil one has had much influence in my life. Many, as they have read the opening story in the Holy Bible have convicted Eve of all that is wrong in the world. Heck the truth is many men in the world lay all the blame of everything at her feet. Perhaps that is why many of them, those that have yet to find themselves in Christ, think their role in life is to be what I like to call "The Punisher".

I think a woman's biggest obstacle in life is that sometimes we think way too much and, ironically at the same time, we willingly trust too quickly.

The evil one is shrewd. If he has tricked you, then you must forgive Eve for being connived in the beginning. I can't even fathom what life was like in the very beginning. I believe that Satan was a trusted friend to Eve. Logically, they were only warned to stay away from the Tree of Knowledge. I have never read about a warning to Eve or Adam about the serpent. Have you?

What I am saying is simply this, "Forgive yourself for all your mistakes, even if in your heart you KNEW better before committing them. And once you nail all that junk to the cross, understand God already forgave you for that and everything else you are going to do 'wrong' until the day you die!"

We walk in the flesh my friends. It is why we are warned in Ephesians to wear our spiritual armor daily for we are in the midst of a Spiritual Battle every day! The Bible is our go to advice for all the troubles this fallen world has to throw at us. It is

14

God's Word. Read it daily for protection.

The evil one has already amped up the fear machine and pointed it in my direction. I will pray for protection and strength daily as I reveal who I was.

I know in my heart that God has protected me from absolute destruction my entire life. I know with His strength; I will be able to walk through the fire.

He loves me as He also Loves You. Jesus, His only begotten son carried the cross for all of us. Remember what God said about Jesus when John the Baptist baptized Jesus in the Jordan River? From Mathew, Chapter 3, verse 17:

> and behold, a voice out of the heavens said, "This is My Beloved Son, in whom I am well-pleased." (Matthew 3:17, NASB)

I hope you come to understand that when you accept Jesus Christ as your Lord and Savior, Christ is in you. Therefore, when God looks at you, He says the same thing. He is pleased with you!

With that reminder stated as much for myself as all who take the time to read my story, I take a deep breath of Faith and leap off the ledge:

My first memory of others praying over me dates back to the 3rd or 4th year of my life. It is how I developed my deep distaste for 7up.

Soda was something I never got. I needed to take medicine that I hated and my reward was an entire can of 7up.To this day 7up tastes like that awful medicine to me. My pills were crushed because I could barely swallow. My tonsils were so huge they were closing the passage of air to my lungs.

The gist was my life was in danger. People were praying for me. I am sure it was my Aunt Janet's prayers that were the most impressive. She never failed to awe me with her strength.

Obviously, my life was saved, for here I am 40 years later sharing my incredible journey with you!

My first memory of praying to God on my own behalf would be somewhere around the 7th or 8th year of my life. I was spending the summer with my father and step mother.

Have you ever heard that saying, "Do as I say, not as I do."? Yea, I kind of thought you might have. As many parents did back then, our parents smoked. My brother who is only 10 months and 10 days younger than me had grabbed some smokes and a lighter and invited me to join him for some fun.

At the time my father lived in a stilt cabin located in a park with all the amenities. We went down to the swings and he lit the first one and gave it to me. We hung out laughing and being kids and of course smoking those cigarettes. We didn't inhale the smoke, but we knew we were cool! Our stepmother was observing us out of the window. We headed home not knowing we had been caught.

When we came inside, we quickly knew we had been busted. Chris made us go to our bedroom and we knew the punishment was about to begin. She informed us if we wanted to smoke we were going to smoke like adults. We learned how to inhale that summer day. She wasn't having any of this silliness with puffing she explained! One after another she lit them for us so we could get that first deep inhale correctly. I think it was on the 3rd full cigarette that I began throwing up.

Tommy and I were both promising we'd never smoke again. She pushed it a little further, but finally left us in our room to wait for our father to come home so she could inform him of our improper behavior. You see, we weren't only caught smoking. We were also in trouble for theft!

To this day, I don't know if my father actually beat my brother's butt or not. I just know I was terrified by the sound coming out of the front room. I swear to you; that stilt cabin was shaking! I was trembling with fear! I was also on the brink of tears.

My step mother had me in the kitchen with her. Tommy, being the one who confessed to taking the cigarettes, was the first to go before our father. To this day I am amazed at the advice she gave me. You see, as I write this book, my step mother does not believe in God or His only begotten son. I think I am the only one allowed to praise God without repercussion around her simply because she cannot deny this story!

With that being said she looked at me and said, "Your only chance of not being spanked is to pray to God to save you."

I don't know if I've said a more passionate heartfelt prayer than my very first one, but I promise you it is the passionate ones that have been answered in the most obvious ways. My biggest signs from God have followed my most heartfelt prayers. That is not to say I have always gotten what I have prayed for! What I have received are answers and signs meant to provide me with relief or guidance.

When I went before my father, he looked at me for a moment. I was so terrified I began begging to be forgiven and I was a mess! My father simply said, "Wendy, I don't know why I'm not going to spank you but I'm not. Something is telling me it is not needed."

I knew what that something was! God had saved me! I was blown away even as a child by this God. My father was not someone to

17

tangle with back then or even today for that matter! Back then he was the strongest, smartest, savviest man I knew. Certainly not one to be easily swayed once his mind was made up. When he told me I was off the hook, I just knew God must be truly something to have been able to overcome my father!

Can you imagine for just a moment how cool an event like that would be for a child? From that day forth, God was my Best Friend. I talked to Him like a best friend would talk to their best friend. Some days, I talked to Him for hours! I promised to help any and all He sent my way. I was going to help Him save the world!

You would think with a beginning like that I would NEVER have decided that I could outwit God. However, that is not how my story goes!

I ask you, which of you has not thought you could outwit your parents? Trust me you are not alone when it comes to that thought! I just took that thought a step further. I thought I could outsmart the creator of all!

Today I laugh about that. God and I are chummy again. I know He smiles upon me. I am back to talking to Him daily. Life is so abundant my friends when you grasp the truth. It takes some of us longer than others to get it! Forgive yourself! I am sitting here with a smile on my face. The words have stopped flowing for now. Have a BLESSED day my friends. Our Father loves all of us, even those who have yet to see the truth or hear it!

Wendy, Mom of Many

Chapter Four

The Boy and My Plan to Outwit God!

It was the summer of my 12th year when I decided that maybe God did NOT have the best plan when it came to me and my life. I really had no desire to be a mother. Just that year my own mother had said some hurtful things to me and while she had apologized to me for one of the incidents, it was my fear that I would do the same thing to my children that made me think God did not know what He was doing when it came to His plan for me.

My mom had me when she was 17 years old. She conceived me when she was only 16! She did the best by my brother and me as she could.

So, I was beginning to question why I had to be a mother to many. I did not want children at all in this moment of my life. I now had a baby sister who was 2. While I thought babies were cute, they were a lot of work! I did not know if I had it in me to be a good mom. I decided if I couldn't be a good mom, I didn't want to be a mom at all!

My daily talks with God had become more of questioning, bargaining sessions. It has not escaped me that when you stop seeking God's will in your life, you have a harder time hearing what He has to say. It is like you turn your ears off in a way just because you don't like what he has to say. I decided I needed clear answers and I felt like there was no better place at the time to get those answers than in a church. Funny isn't it.

There were quite a few churches around where I lived. One day, while my brother and I were biking our way to the Riviera Club, I saw one that had a sign out front advertising a youth group. I told my brother the pool could wait. I wanted to check out this youth group.

We rode up into the parking lot and came face to face with a group of three boys on their bikes. The leader of the group of course was the only one brave enough to actually speak. The others just giggled at what he said.

"You can't go inside." He informed me, "This group is not for you." His crew chuckled.

Well, I thought, obviously he did not know who he was messing with! I looked at him and asked, "Who are you to tell me I cannot go into God's house?" I was not frightened.

Just then the youth leader came outside. I chuckle to this day, for I think she was surprised to see five of us there outside the door sitting on our bikes. She informed us that we could come inside. I parked my bike, looked over my shoulder and stuck my tongue out at the "boy" who obviously did not have that much power after all!

Before the study was over, I knew his name and he knew mine. I must admit I was enamored with his green eyes, dark brown incredibly curly hair and the gap in his front teeth. When we were dismissed, we all went back out to our bikes.

I don't think Danny Joe's friends were too happy at all when he asked if my brother and I would like to hang out with him and his friends. I, on the other hand, felt my heart pull.

I was becoming quite smitten on this boy and it was more than obvious that he was feeling something for me.

We walked and talked all day long. My brother and I had to be home at a certain time and I was not into getting into trouble, so, home we had to go.

My brother liked Danny Joe so agreeing to come back the next day was no issue.

That night, while I was floating on a cloud, I also had my looming future ahead of me.

It is my belief that this was the exact moment I hit the age of consent, for this is when I became a genius! I reasoned, with the help of Satan I am sure, there was only one Mary. With that in mind, as long as I refrained from sex, I would not have a baby at a young age.

Resolved in my decision, my plan was formed. Believing that I could keep my plan safely guarded from God, I decided I would have to let Danny Joe know everything. I needed him to agree to my proposal or I could never see him again.

I have to stop now. Reliving all of this is not going to be fun or easy but it is most necessary. I will continue late tonight after my children are asleep. I hope that you realize I am human. Through the chapters of my life, as I share those with you, try to stay away from judging me. It is in my own judging of others and their choices that I have landed in some of the hottest water!

Wendy, Mom of Many

Chapter Five

Face to Face with an Angel

I had to pray on how to proceed with this next chapter. I was not sure how I was to tell this next part for many will not believe. I questioned long and hard, "Am I to share this with the world? People will think I'm crazy, or worse grandiose." It was in realizing the fear I felt that I knew I must share it with the world.

As I have mentioned, my mother and I were not the closest two individuals in the world during this season of my life. I didn't understand why she taunted, insulted and picked on me so much. I just know that I felt she did not love me back then.

Danny Joe and I had become best friends during the course of the year. Prior to this time in my life Tabitha, who started out as my enemy in the 3rd grade, had been my greatest confidant. By age 13 Danny Joe was, beyond a shadow of doubt, my best friend. He knew everything about me including my message from God.

We would go on walks through the woods. We talked about parenting and what we liked and disliked about our own parents. We went down by White River a lot and hung out there. He made me laugh. We honestly enjoyed one other.

When I had first met Danny Joe, I was a whole lot of tomboy without a lot of "girly" qualities. My mother had made so much fun of girls and all they liked that I sought out none of that. It made life simpler. My stepmother encouraged my girl side.

I guess between the two of them I was quite something! (Yes, as you can see even humbleness is a characteristic of mine ~ ha ha)

By age 13, I had played on a softball team and a basketball team for 5 years. Thanks to my stepmother I had taken baton lessons for a summer and had won 5th in the state at a baton competition. I felt way out of my comfort zone in my outfit but secretly it was the prettiest I had ever felt!

So on this particular day, I was going to be meeting Danny Joe after my mother left for work. I had decided I would wear some makeup that day. I had no idea what I was doing, but I was attempting to apply some mascara to my eyelashes when suddenly, my mother was behind me. We locked eyes in the mirror and she said, "I don't know why you're doing that. It's not like you'll ever be pretty."

Now up to that point, my mom had said some cruel things to me and I don't know why that knocked the air out of me, but it did. She walked away and I remember thinking to myself, 'No matter what, it's a parent's job to always tell their children they are beautiful.'

I was so distraught in my heart I can't even put the turmoil I was feeling in my heart into words.

I raised my eyes back up to the mirror and there she was; a beautiful woman I did not recognize, looking at me.

My first thought was not really even a thought. I was blown away by her beauty. I gazed upon her. She said to me, "Wendy, YOU ARE a CHILD of GOD. You ARE BEAUTIFUL!" and she was gone.

I was confused, amazed and suddenly confident in my beauty. I went to my room and waited for my mother to leave for work. I felt so radiant. I just know I was close to glowing!

Once my mom was gone, I watched the clock waiting long enough to make sure she was not coming back. After about

23

twenty minutes, I headed to Danny Joe's house.

Along the way I wondered who the beautiful lady was. I wondered, 'Was she me coming back to tell me how pretty I was going to be?'

I certainly was nothing glamorous right now, but I told myself, 'If that was me in the future, a grown up version of me, I am going to be flat out BEAUTIFUL!'

I pondered this, 'If that was me, a grown up version of me, when did I get all that lovely curly hair?'

Oh how hard I am laughing at myself as I write this. Recently I have wondered if I'd of known back then that the girl in the mirror was an angel, how my life would have played out. I only realized that I had come face to face with an angel right before I conceived my second to last child, but I digress, I am getting ahead of myself!

When I arrived at Danny's house, his dad opened the door. I asked if Danny Joe was there and indeed he was! He came smiling into the room and I walked over to him smiling. He grabbed my hand and turned to his dad and asked if we could go for a walk.

Danny's dad looked at me and him and said to Danny that he didn't know what it was about me but he knew Danny Joe better hold on tight to me. Danny Joe squeezed my hand and his dad told him that I was a keeper. My heart soared. In one day I was called both beautiful and a keeper! That was when I thought for sure it was going to be me and Danny Joe for life.

** How I came to know that the woman I saw in the mirror that day was not me at some point in the future happened right before I conceived Delilah. A friend of mine who I worked with was researching history during our lunch break at work. She called me over to her computer to see this picture of a female version of Arch Angel Gabriel that an artist had painted centuries ago. I almost fell out of my chair. That artist had captured her! My messenger was an angel!

How do you tell someone that? The answer is you don't. At least I didn't. Not right away. I can tell you this, I was astonished. I began to question everything. It brought pangs of massive guilt as well as a million questions.

You see, the last conversation I had one on one with God was right as everything was beginning to get really ugly for me. I had told Him I wanted to help all the struggling moms in the world find hope. I had come to the conclusion that they all needed hope.

I reminded God that I really did not want this whole "mom of many" life. I questioned Him asking why He couldn't just turn me into a famous author. I shared with Him were I to become famous, I would have all I needed to help everyone! I reasoned with him reminding him that my teachers all thought I was pretty good at writing! Even my school mates had predicted that I would be a famous poet. I wrote all the time!

I thought it was a great plan myself. That, my friend, was mere weeks before everything in my world turned upside down. As I close out this chapter, I ask for your prayers. I pray for strength and focus to accomplish the task that I have been given. I request that any believer pray for me. Pray for strength and protection. Praying for others carries more weight than praying for yourself!

Be blessed and be a blessing, Wendy, Mom of Many

Chapter Six

If You Love Someone You Must Be Willing to Let Them Go!

I joke around with keeping things simple in my forties for fear I may lose my mind as I get older!

Memories get dusty when we don't look at them for decades. This was the case for me when it came to Danny Joe. It was on my 41st Birthday that God convicted me. He used Danny Joe as the vehicle to drive me back in time.

I was forced to dive deep and made to recall things I had stuffed away and pretended were non-existent. I apologize for the hazy recall. I have come to believe since there is still a little haze around the fine details that those are not the most important ones, and I finally moved beyond them to the main gist of my story.

Something happened before the 8th grade. I don't know if it was that Danny Joe was going to go live with his mom because his dad and he were not getting along or what. It's just the last time I saw him until the next time I saw him again, this is what I said to myself as I walked home, "When you love someone you must be willing to let them go." Today, I know those words came from God.

It was okay I assured myself as I walked back home. This next school year I was going to be so busy, I wouldn't have time to just hang with Danny Joe after school anyway. I was going to be on the basketball team again. Besides, I really wanted to win The Best Christian Award that they had held out like a golden carrot to all of us in the 7th grade. So, not being distracted by my friendship that had soared to great heights would be a good thing.

Danny Joe had taught me how to kiss over the summer. I had never felt so loved by someone then I felt when I was in his arms.

So, here I was in the 8th grade at a private catholic school going for The Best Christian Award. The irony makes me laugh today. Why didn't they call it The Best Catholic Award?

I studied hard. I impressed my teachers. Our team was having an incredible basketball season. I even received a handshake from the coach of another team! He told me he had never seen a girl play ball like me! I was elected to be on the committee that was going to write who we were all going to become when we grew up. Hands down everyone knew I was going to be a famous writer. I talked in rhyme most of the time. You could say I was a female version of Dr. Seuss only I did not make up silly words to rhyme, I told complete stories in rhyme.

You can always tell when I am in tune with the Holy Spirit. If I'm not writing and rhyming something is wrong! At this time in my life I was completely focused!

It was late winter of that school year when a couple of boys on bikes were racing around our school. Like school kids, we all rushed to the windows to see what the racket was all about. One of the boys was yelling, "I've come back for you! Do you see? I've come back for you!"

I knew that voice! It was Danny Joe! How I kept my feet on the floor when my heart was soaring so high is beyond me. I shot off a quick prayer for his safety as they announced over the loud speaker that all students needed to get back into their seats. They were sending someone out in an attempt to grab the trouble makers!

I was elated and worried all at the same time. Getting over to Ravenswood to see Danny Joe was not going to happen that day.

I had basketball practice after school and it would be dark before I got home.

I prayed that he would understand when I didn't show up after school. It wasn't like he had my phone number to call. I was not allowed to give it out. My mom was only allowed 25 calls a month due to her phone plan. I was allowed none!

I assured myself he would know in his heart that I wanted to be with him. How could he not know how much I loved him?

I did not get over to his side of Keystone Avenue until the weekend. When I went by his house no one was home. I hung around the neighborhood just walking where we used to walk with each other and that is when I met Debbie.

We only hung out with each other for a few short weeks before school let out. When the opportunity struck over the next few weeks, I crossed under Keystone Avenue and hung out with her. I was always secretly hoping I'd run into Danny Joe. It never happened that summer.

The school year was finally at a close. My brother had been shipped off to live with my father in the last couple of months of the school year due to being kicked out of school. I was so excited. A whole summer with Danny Joe and no brother following me everywhere I went.

At my graduation I won so many awards it was crazy. Amazing what you can accomplish when you are focused on the Lord and walking in the spirit! I also won the one award I was going for; The Best Christian Award was mine! Who knew it also came with a $35? Bonus!!

When I went over to meet Debbie that day, Danny Joe was still nowhere to be found. The weekend was coming and I just knew he'd be at his dad's.

With Debbie's help, we formed a plan for us to be able to stay the weekend together without either of us being accountable to our parents! I knew it was wrong, purposely deceiving my mother. Regardless, lie I did. I asked my mom if I could spend the night at Debbie's house and she asked her mom if she could spend the night with me. Not the greatest plan in the world, but it worked.

I took my $35 with me. Debbie and I convinced an adult to purchase us two little bottles of Canadian Mist and a six pack of beer. I had never drunk before then but Debbie assured me it was the best!

We hung out with friends and played some kind of ball game in the street. I'm a little fuzzy on how the whole drinking thing got started. The beer was nasty. Debbie assured me I wouldn't even notice the taste once I'd had a little Jack. I took a sip. "OH! Nastier!" I exclaimed.

I don't know whose idea it was for us to race each other by drinking our bottle in one attempt but we did. We were so drunk that night. I don't know how I lived through it. By 5:00 A.M. we were ready to crash.

There was no way could we go to my house. Debbie said her mom would never notice when we came in so, we went there. I was worried that when her mom got up, she would smell the alcohol on our breath. I knew that the smell of alcohol came from your stomach and not your mouth. After sharing this valuable information with Debbie, we decided to eat an entire box of Oreo cookies as well as swallow a little mouthwash and toothpaste. I

promise you, it was not easy on the stomach! We checked out each other's breath and we were sure we'd never be discovered. We went to lie down.

I don't know how long we were asleep when Debbie's mother came into her room, woke us up, and informed us that the neighbor had busted us. In a gist, Debbie's mom had called my mom. The game was up. Debbie's mom dropped me off at my house. She apologized to my mom informing her that she was sure it was Debbie who had been the leader. I wasn't that worried until my mother informed me that my father was on his way to come get me. She was sending me to live with him for good. I couldn't believe it. One mistake and I'm gone I thought? My brother pulled stunts like this time and time again before she sent him off!

Things were just about to change dramatically in my world. My sifting was about to truly begin!

I had and have had no idea how and what I was going to write about next. I have had no clue as to how I was to precede after my previous chapter and again here I am at the end of another chapter of my life! I hope I am not boring you with the details. I think it's important for you to know I'm no better than anyone. I too have been stumbling through this thing we call life. It is my job to help you see the Glory of God. If I accomplish that I will have fulfilled my purpose and nothing in the world could be better than that!

Be blessed and be a blessing!

Wendy, Mom of Many!

Chapter Seven

Grounded for Losing My Virginity!

When I ended my last chapter, I closed my computer crying. Over this next year of my life, so many things happened. I was praying to God, asking Him to help me with how to start the next chapter.

You see, I cannot seem to be capable of writing the next chapter of my story until I hear the title for it. So, here I was on my way to a fellowship gathering with ladies that I attend service with each Sunday. Honestly, I was scared to death to go because I didn't really know a lot of them. I was at the entrance of the housing addition and I had pulled over to flip on the inner light in the car so I could read the rest of the directions when God spoke to me.

I still have the evil one messing with me and my confidence every day. I have a suspension he is always searching for a perfect way to pounce. If he even gets a hint of fear, he's on it! Anyway, all of a sudden I heard it, the title to this chapter. I was surprised at first and then I burst into a healthy bout of laughter.

If I haven't mentioned it before, God is humorous. Seeing how Jesus says if we know him we know the father, it only makes sense that God would be humorous for Jesus is!

I needed that laughter. Along with it came the knowledge that I would be okay. So, what the heck, here we go!

I barely had time to grasp the fact that my mother was shipping me off to my father's on the pretense that I was "too much to handle" when I heard my father's car pull in the drive way. This was crazy! I had begged and pleaded to live with my father and had been told NO again and again. Now I was going to be sent there for staying out all night. She hadn't even waited to hear my side of the story. She had an opportunity to make me look bad and I just felt in my heart she was happy things had worked out this way.

She could get rid of me and not look like it was because she was not close to me. Honestly I felt she barely knew who I truly was.

I don't know what my mom said to my dad on the phone, but he was hot. He yelled at me to pack my stuff. No longer was I 'Wendy, Honor roll student, Best Christian, all around good kid.' I was in major trouble.

I don't know why I was attacked so viciously, but my father was in my face demanding to know what I had done. I was so terrified by his anger I could not tell him I had been drinking. I told him I'd just hung out with Debbie. Nothing more, nothing less.

I was called a liar. I was marched out of the house with two trash bags full of all I owned and then driven in silence to Westfield. My head was pounding and I just wanted the day to be over. I felt like I was trapped in a nightmare.

I was sent to my room while they decided my fate. Since I had denied doing anything wrong, I wasn't sure exactly what that punishment would be. I fell asleep waiting for them to come get me. When they woke me up I swear I thought my head was going to explode. To this day it remains the worst hangover I have ever had. I couldn't let them know how bad I felt for they might realize I'd been drinking and until my charges were handed down by my new found prison guards, I had no idea just how low they thought of me.

They were 100% positive that I had lost my virginity and for that

I was going to be grounded for the summer as well as the first part of the school year! I was astounded. I denied it until I was blue in the face. That didn't matter. They were convinced even more so by my denial that I had slept with some boy.

As my step-mother used to say, 'if you aren't guilty there is no need for a defense.' I even had my rear end beat repeatedly for a crime I did not commit.

"Why is this happening?" I questioned God.

It was probably my anger at my circumstance that kept me from hearing an answer. It was the first time I could remember feeling like God was no longer listening to me when I called out to Him.

My fate was sealed. I would work at the family construction company. I would earn minimum wage. I could play softball and basketball as long as I paid for the expenses and I was being signed up for marching band!

The best part about being involved with marching band was it was expensive and I was being held responsible for those costs as well. That one threw me for a loop! I'd played a clarinet in the 6th grade for music class. I didn't even remember a single note let alone the scale! As if all of that were not enough, I also had to budget my book rental and school lunch fees as well as have a fund for unexpected school expenses. The reasoning behind having me pay for everything was so that I would appreciate it that much more.

My step mother, who for some reason was playing soft ball herself, but had not bought herself a mitt yet, was thrilled to discover that my glove fit her hand. Since she wasn't sure she was going to join the team she was subbing for as a regular, she was not interested in buying herself a glove yet. I think it was my 4th night there that we went and watched her play as a family.

33

When the game was over and we had met back up, I questioned where my glove was? Chris had mistakenly left it in the dugout. Of course when she went back to get it, it was gone. She didn't even act like it was a big deal. I had had that glove since the first grade! When my mom first bought it and gave it to me it was ridiculously big. By the time I was in the 6th grade, it was like an extension of my hand. There wasn't a ball I couldn't catch with that glove. I was physically sick to my stomach over the loss.

When I was asking if Chris knew what the cost was for joining the high school softball team, she informed me that since I needed to budget in the cost of a new glove, it was looking like that would not be a wise investment of time or money. I was astounded. I did not lose my glove, SHE did! There was no arguing that point. No use in even trying. I resolved that I would at least be able to play basketball in the fall.

Over the summer I taught myself how to play the clarinet. Surprisingly, I liked marching band. Some of the greatest high school memories I have involve band camp and band competitions.

I hated having Chris for a boss though. She loved it a bit too much. She would have me filling pot holes in the driveway during storms when even the guys were being sent home. No better time to see where gravel was needed than in the rain she would tell me.

The worst chore she gave me was pulling weeds. I informed her there was an area of poison ivy and I would not be able to work in that area. Who knew she'd have me dress in pants, a long sleeve shirt to protect my arms and gloves on an 80 to 90 degree day! Needless to say I ended up with poison ivy everywhere including in my throat and my eyes. It was so bad; I ended up in the bathroom one night with a razor. I shaved every part of my body and then I doused myself in rubbing alcohol. I think I still needed a shot. For sure I took those little white pills.

I was absolutely miserable. I started out my freshman year of high school knowing a few girls from band and looking like the ultimate pizza face! Acne has nothing on poison ivy!

Regardless, I had made it through the summer and basketball was around the corner. I loved that sport. The coach had us running a lot and I decided it would be in my best interest to build up my stamina so I began running a few miles while dribbling my basketball to take my mind off of running.

This particular Saturday morning, I managed to rip a contact while putting it in my eye. I didn't want to deal with a long lecture from Chris about how irresponsible I was for tearing my contact and how replacing it would affect my budget. I just wanted to get out of the house and have a little time to myself to talk to God.

I was on my way back home, less than 2/10 of a mile from our driveway when I recognized the Compton's vehicle as they drove by. I got back out in the middle of the road and squinted. I could see a station wagon on the west side of the road. I thought to myself, 'Must be the grandfather of the girl who lived in the house after the woods.' He was always mushroom hunting.

Because I had one good eye and one bad eye, for the most part, I was looking down just in front of me. I heard a male voice ahead of me call out, "Playing ball?"

I looked up and stopped dead in my tracks with my hand in midair. I think the ball made contact with my hand one more time, but I failed to shove it back down.

I heard it thump again and again as it thumped off the road. A naked man was a couple of yards in front of me and he was pointing a gun directly at me. I was frozen.

The night before on the news, there was a story about a few girls that had been found raped and murdered and left naked in fields. I screamed out to God in my head "This is not how I die! I haven't accomplished anything yet!" I was shocked, confused, and admittedly terrified.

The naked man approached me. He shoved the nozzle of a gun into my stomach and said, "I'll kill you if you move."

With his other hand, he reached out to touch me. I do not know what made me say, "Oh my here comes my father!", but I said it.

He barely glanced over his shoulder and that is when I went to step around him. He caught me and he punched me with that gun right in the stomach. "Little girl I will kill you if you lie to me again." he growled.

By the grace of God, his face changed from hatred to terror and he ran from me, jumped in his car, and sped off.

Suddenly, there was Mrs. Compton asking if I was okay. I couldn't even talk. I think she told me to go home. Honestly I don't know.

I never retrieved that ball. I came crashing into the house through the screen door. Cady, my baby sister, was on Chris' lap and they both looked at me. Chris asked me what the heck was wrong with me. I was a visible mess. I can't fathom what I must have looked like. All I could say was, "Guy, guy, guy, gun, gun, gun, me, me, me".

She asked me if I was making up a lie and I think I screamed. My sister will confirm that to this day, this is the clearest memory from her childhood. She claims she can still smell my sweat.

Gross, I know.

The police were called. I was given a soda for its sugar. I was spiking a fever, a high fever due to my shock. When the police arrived the main one that talked to me was a volunteer sheriff. He was also the driving instructor that was in the car with the Carmel High School Students whose lives were cut short on SR 38 due to a collision with a 7up truck. He was the one that informed my parents that I was in shock and insisted they give me a soda pop immediately.

My own mom wasn't even called to my knowledge. If she was, she did not come to see me.

All I wanted to do was get in the shower. Finally, I was allowed to do so. When the hot water ran out, I dried off and went to my room to die.

My father and step mother don't know, but I heard their argument. It was the only time in my life that I know beyond a shadow of doubt, Chris argued for me.

My father, in a gist, said he didn't understand the big deal. After all, he justified, I wasn't really raped. He continued on, suggesting that it should not be that big of a deal based on their belief that I was not even a virgin. "She probably brought this on herself." My father claimed.

I closed my eyes and cried myself to sleep. These people raising me were so clueless as to who I truly was and what I was about. I was devastated.

My stomach remained bruised for over two weeks. He'd gotten me pretty darn good for an old guy.

Some of you reading this will respect the fact that this chapter has left me exhausted. I thought I'd get farther than I did but I must stop here. I am crying too hard to go on. This is just the beginning of my story. The good news is, I am here to share it with you and I promise it has a happy ending.

Be blessed and be a blessing,

Wendy, Mom of Many

Chapter Eight

Too Angry to Process the Assault with Love

I warn you to guard yourself from allowing anger to be the leading emotion in your life. First it blinds you, then, it allows you to become self-righteous. There is a time for anger but it is short lived and rarely sweet. Please, if you get nothing else out of this story of mine, get that.

Anger is one of many footholds the evil one needs to have entrance into your heart. You do not want him even getting close to that! So, when you feel anger coming on, I urge you to get down on your knees and give that to God. That looks different than "Giving it to God."

Let me see if I can somehow elaborate on this through my story. Let's begin with this:

Footnotes and Fill-ins from my previous chapter: *Grounded for losing my virginity*

1. Yes I was grounded for something I did not do, BUT I did misbehave.

2. My punishment did not fit the crime, BUT I brought the trouble on myself by disobeying, lying and breaking rules I knew were not meant to be broken.

3. I was angry at God for allowing such an awful thing to happen to me.

4. As a child and here in my telling, I did not give sufficient praise for the amazing story Mrs. Compton shared.

4 deserves more details. It was while I was losing my mind due to being questioned if I was making this entire assault up by Chris, remember, I couldn't talk, "Guy, guy, guy, gun, gun, gun, me, me, me", was literally all I could say. I could not say anything else. I could barely form those words; anyway, that is when Mrs. and Mr. Compton came to the door. Mrs. Compton was very worried about me. I could hear it in her voice. She asked Chris if I'd told her what happened. I can't remember what Chris said. The numbness was taking over. I heard her tell Chris she was so mad at herself for not insisting louder that they turn around. When they had pulled in their driveway, she shared the fact that she just couldn't get out. She insisted they go back and make sure I was okay. God told her she must. She had obeyed.

Now I am so thankful that God was watching out for me because that whole thing could have been so much worse. I may not have made it out alive. As it was, I was barely touched. Some women have stories that will leave you in absolute tears over their pain.

When they raced off, I didn't realize it was to get this man. He lost them on a high speed chase on the back roads she informed my step mother. He didn't have a license plate on the car so there was nothing more than a description of the car and my description of the man for the police to go on. I couldn't tell the police anything more than he was old and naked and his hand not holding the gun had a flaw. I didn't tell any of them he'd punched me with the gun. They might want to look at me and there was no way I could bare that.

It was through reliving this event that I realized that this amazing woman had listened to God. God told her to go back for me and she refused to get out of the car until they did just that.

I was in shock when that was all revealed the first time. I was far from able to comprehend. My vital signs were proof of that.

By the time I got in my room I wanted to die and that was the state I was in when I heard my father's cruel assessment of the situation. I was angered and insulted by his words.

When anger is your leading emotion you are headed for trouble. It clouds your mind. It closes off part of your heart. It can and will cause you so much more trouble. You HAVE to let it go for your own protection. Ask God for help even if it is Him you are angry with.

It is okay to talk to God and share how you feel. He will help you heal if you reach out to Him. Sadly, it is in our anger that we lose confidence in His mighty power. It is mighty because through Him all things can be done. If somehow you have interpreted His mighty power to be a destructive force, you do not know the Father. He does all things through LOVE. We are just confused by the whole "fear God" line. The fear as in to be afraid of comes from the evil one I believe. God LOVES YOU. He LOVES ALL OF US! There is not a rational reason to be afraid of Him. To truly be 'In Fear of God' means more awe than actual Fear. A total realm of respect. An honoring kind of fear.

So, there I was on my way back to school. I felt empty, lost, and alone. I was too ashamed to share what had happened to me with anyone. I walked into my biology class and sat in my seat. Everyone shuffled into the room and then the bell rang.

Mr. Denari, one of my favorite teachers ever, was not at his desk. When his substitute walked in, I could not breathe. My heart was pounding in my chest so hard I could hear it.

Everyone else was happy to see him. They called him ABC goldfish. Now, to me, he was my perpetrator. He looked like him. The guy that molested me had something wrong with the hand that wasn't holding his gun. It was semi locked in a position is the best way I can describe it. It was the only odd thing about him

41

that I remembered.

I had no desire to see if this substitute teacher would reveal a handicapped hand. I was engulfed in panic and all I could think about was getting out of that room. I couldn't sit in my seat a moment longer. I stood up and blurted out some excuse and bolted out of the room without waiting for a reply.

Mrs. Compton must have warned her son to keep an eye on me because if memory serves me right, I think he came out of the room and followed me. I stopped and turned and said, "You know don't you?"

He didn't say a word as to what he knew or didn't know. I begged him to tell no one. I somehow don't think that was necessary. In my heart I know his mother had covered that subject with him.

I never wanted to go to court. I did not ever want to relive what had happened. There was no way I could ever get "justice" for what he did to me. I thought I was going to share more of my story but I have no more to say at the moment. This was what He wanted me to share with you in this chapter.

It is my prayer for you that you begin to open yourself up if you are a non-believer. Dig deep into where your disbelief stems from. Try to discover when your mistrust of God formed. It takes courage to acknowledge you KNOW God personally. We live in a world of self-empowerment. You my friend are nothing more than a vapor. When you realize the truth of that and then realize God is right here with you, that He resides IN YOU, you will be able to begin living an abundant life!

Much Love, Wendy, Mom of Many

Chapter Nine

Taking Control of My Destiny

Sliding back to age 14 is not easy. I am amazed how when I sit down to type in the title that has come to me, the words seem to almost fly out onto paper.

The school year had just started; I was in band. I'd been assaulted. I could not stand to hear the thump of a basketball. It was my freshman year. If you can imagine, I was a little withdrawn around home. My grounding had been reduced a little. I was still not allowed to go visit my mother. I was beginning to believe I'd never see Danny Joe again. We had always agreed if we were meant to be, we would be. When he had moved, I had set him free. Granted he'd come back for me, but since I never saw him since that date, I was not convinced he was waiting around for me.

In my heart, I had come to believe that if God wanted me to have a baby my stupid plan to keep from having one was just that; Stupid. I had woken up to just how cruel this world was.

At this moment of my life, I had NOT processed my attack. Nope. Instead, I had processed everything in this way, "I am a virgin, and they think I'm not. Why would they think that? Just because I stayed out all night? Stupid. I guess if I don't do things God's way, he'll send someone to rape me."

That would bring us to Christmas break. I cannot for the life of me remember how it came to be but I was going to be allowed to

go to my mother's for Christmas. I was only going to be able to stay for one night. They didn't tell me in advance. I imagine it was so I would have no time for plans. It was weird that they let me go because she had to work and was going to be gone at night for her shift.

Just like in the old days, I waited. This time I waited for a full thirty minutes before I headed out the door and across Keystone Avenue. Initially I thought her having to go to work might be a trap. When she didn't come back, I left. I walked to the old neighborhood down to where Danny Joe had lived with his dad. My heart stopped as I rounded the corner. His house was gone. GONE! I was dumbfounded. For a moment I just stood in the road. I wasn't ready to go home yet and I thought I'd find Debbie before giving up. My plan was to see if she knew anything. I walked over to her side of the neighborhood. As I got closer to Debbie's house, I ran into some kids I remembered and asked if they knew what had happened to Danny Joe's house and if they'd seen him lately. They informed me he lived in a house down the road and around the corner. They gave me a basic description. One of them told me he was at his Dad's for Christmas. Now my heart was really pounding. I knocked on a couple of wrong doors by their description and then I knocked on the right one.

There was a pool table in one room and a dart board on the wall. When I arrived there, they were in the middle of a game. Danny Joe kept looking at me and smiling at me while he played. I let him know I needed to talk to him about something really serious and when the game was over he cleared the room.

 I told him my mom had sent me off for staying out all night right after school had let out for the year and that I'd been grounded for losing my virginity and he laughed. He laughed so hard that I began to giggle with him. I told him I'd been grounded ever since

the day I had gone to live with my father and since I'd been grounded for supposedly losing my virginity, it was my belief that I should at least do the crime.

44

He argued with me. He reminded me of the promise he'd made. I told him I had changed my mind; that made him laugh. I pushed harder. I questioned him, asking him if he was denying me because I was not pretty enough for him anymore?

He assured me that was not the case. He reminded me it was his job to deny me. He had made a promise to me.

That's when I told him about me being molested and I cried to him and said, "Danny Joe if I don't do things God's way, He'll just send someone to rape me. I want to have a choice in who I give myself to. Please forget about the promise. I need you to help me".

That did it. He took me into some part of the room with some kind of bed in it. I can't remember much other than how much it hurt. I also remember freaking out because blood had gotten on stuff, and I clearly remember how kind he was when it was all over.

The last thing he said to me, until the next time we saw each other again, was at his front door. If I recall one of his 1/2 brothers was standing beside him. Anyway, as I was preparing to exit the house, he looked at me with a grin and said, "You are prettier without all that black around your eyes."

I laughed. I'd put on eye liner and mascara while I was killing time waiting to see if my mom was coming back. According to Danny Joe, I was prettier without any makeup on at all.

When school started again, I shared the fact I'd lost my virginity with Tami. She and I had quickly become great friends. We rode the bus together and it seemed she and I had a lot in common.

She confided some things to me about her life, and I confided some things about my life to her. I still wrote some things in my

45

diary back then, and I had written about Tami. I had also written about me giving up my virginity.

My grounding had been lifted and I was even allowed to invite a friend over for the night. Of course I picked Tami.

Her mom dropped her off at my house. My parents were going out for the night and I can't recall where Tommy and Cady were, maybe they went with Chris and Dad. Anyway, Tami and I had a blast. We went into the kitchen to make some chocolate chip cookies. In the midst of adding the ingredients, I'm not sure which one of us flipped the first bit of flour at whom, but next thing I knew we were in a flour war! It was quite the scene. We finally got the cookies in the oven, cleaned up our mess and we sat down to watch a true story about the first high school female quarterback. I could be wrong but I think her name might have been Tamara. Seeing how that was Tami's real first name, we thought it was cool how a girl she shared names with was a true life mover and shaker. That was right before everything that could go wrong went wrong.

I'm still to this day not sure what made Chris climb up on my bed on that fateful day and fumble through the books on my shelf and find my diary. All I know for sure is I had gotten home from school and there she was waiting for me. She had my diary. I was in trouble. For what you might ask. I was in big big big trouble for losing my virginity; again.

I found it so ironic that nothing was mentioned about how they had been wrong when they accused me of losing my virginity.

Not a single apology regarding calling me a liar for denying I had slept with a boy. No. Just that I was in trouble for it AGAIN!

What happened next was not what I was expecting. Honestly, I never saw it coming. She informed me that this was going to be our secret. My sleeping with Danny Joe would remain between us. She was going to keep my diary for collateral and I was going to baby sit my baby sister every other weekend for free so that she and my father could have some adult time without breaking the bank for a sitter.

As long as I kept my side of the bargain without giving her any trouble, she would keep this information to herself and not share it with my father. That was acceptable to me. I didn't want anyone to know. My dad already thought the worst of me. I reasoned that there was no need to add to that.

I'm not sure why Chris shared the information with my Grandmother, but she did. On one of my free weekends, I was sent to my grandma's house to spend the night there. I figured it was a way they could get rid of me and have an eye kept on me at the same time. I didn't know until I got there what Chris had done.

My grandma drove us to the store and had a conversation with me about boys. She told me Chris had wanted to share my diary with both my grandma and grandpa, but they didn't have any desire to read it, so she had told them what I had done.

I wanted to climb into a well and stay there. That night when my grandpa had gone to lie down, he'd asked to talk to me. I sat down on the edge of his bed and he grabbed my hand and said, "Wendy, that witch could tell us you murdered someone and we'd still love you. You know that right?" I laughed and said to him, "I know it now."

My Grandpa Duke is no longer in this world but I love him so much for that comment.

When I went home I was so mad at Chris. She had lied. She talked about how important being honest was and here she had flat out lied to me. That weekend I decided I had to get my diary back as soon as possible.

The next weekend it was my turn to watch Cady. I decided it was my turn to ransack her room. I was going to find my diary and take it back! I did not find it that weekend but I was not done looking. That next weekend was a school dance and I was excited because it fell on my weekend. Right before the weekend came Chris informed me she was going to need me to baby-sit Cady. I was visibly upset. I reminded her that I had just watched Cady last weekend.

"This weekend is mine. You promised I could have every other weekend off." I said.

She smirked at me and asked if I'd like my father to read my diary.

I offhandedly said to her, "Sure, go ahead. I really don't care at this point." She'd already told my grandparents. I truly didn't care anymore.

That's when she threw me for a loop. "Okay" she calmly replied, "You should know I'll also have to pick up the phone and call Tami's dad."

My heart lurched. I'd forgotten that I'd written some things about Tami in my diary. She had me. No way could I allow her to do that. I caved but my heart was longing to smash Chris. Oh, I was so mad. What would make a person do something like that I wondered.

I resolved myself to finding my diary during my next opportunity no matter what. I had to get it back. Who knew while searching for it, I was going to find dirt on Chris. As soon as I realized that was what I had found while searching for my diary, I knew I was going to use it if I needed to. It was the one sure fire way I was going to be able to get my hands back on my diary or so that is what I thought.

I'd had that diary since I was 10 years old and she was using it as a weapon against me. Now, I had something to hold over her head; A letter from a friend of hers. I knew she didn't want the world to see what that had to say. I tucked it away for safe keeping.

The following weekend arrived and I thought it was going to be my weekend. It only made sense that it would be my weekend because I had now watched Cady two weekends in a row.

However, in my step mother's new found confidence in her threat to share my diary with Tami's father as a viable weapon to keep me in line and under her thumb, she had decided I would be no longer be any trouble in the baby sitting department. She'd found my weakness; my loyalty to my friend.

I'll never forget her face and how it changed as our conversation progressed after I had initially told her I wasn't going to baby-sit Cady that third weekend in a row.

She said, "Well, I guess I'll call Tami's dad."

I looked at her and said, "Fine. You do that. I guess tomorrow I'll begin sharing with the world your letter from your friend in the Bahamas."

If looks could kill, I'd be dead. I cheered myself on in my head. "Sucks to have someone threaten you like that doesn't it?" I asked already knowing the answer.

I like to believe she decided that blackmail wasn't really kind. I was surprised by the following chain of events as they unfolded that fateful day.

I never thought she would not allow me to have my diary back. She told me I had taught her a lesson all right. It was a lesson I didn't see coming really. She told me that lesson was, 'Don't keep things in writing that you wouldn't be okay with someone else reading.'

I said that I agreed. That was something I was never going to do again.

She went into her room and brought my diary back. Still, she refused to give it to me. She said to me, "Get my letter. We are going to burn them at the same time."

Now I was the one caught off guard. Truly I was panicked. That diary had a lot in it. I didn't want it burnt!!!!

No matter what I said, she was not backing down. She was going to burn my diary. I got the letter and at the same time we tossed our respective 'blackmail' items into the fire.

I was sick. I wanted to puke. For an instant I think I even hated her.

That diary was supposed to go to my first child. The daughter I had been told would be born first. I told myself, "Never again." I was not going to write about anything or about anyone that could hurt someone again.

I cried myself to sleep that night over my loss. My father never knew about this incident. It wasn't like I could tell him.

Well, here I am again, out of words. That was hard but not near as hard as the last chapter.

I had dealt with a lot of this guilt when God convicted me on my 41st birthday. Until my next chapter, I say to you, "Be kind to others. Don't blackmail. Keep secrets. Don't gossip."

Wendy, Mom of Many

Chapter Ten

In Defense of My Step-Mother

Throughout my story I don't want people to get the wrong idea about how I feel towards all my parents. I LOVE Them. Yes, throughout my life you will see mistakes they made in both judgment and discipline. Who among us can say any different?

Chris pushed me like the military pushes its soldiers. I thank her for her training. She gave me so many tools. I honestly don't think I'd be as well rounded had she not been a major influence in my life.

In reading my story from the beginning you know that Chris is the one that got me to say my first prayer. How can you stay angry at someone who helps you get closer to God? The short and simple answer is, "You Can't". A relationship with Our Father should be your number one goal in this life.

As it says in Matthew 6:33:

> But seek first His kingdom and His righteousness, and all these things will be added to you. (Matthew 6:33, NASB)

So to me Chris was a great teacher who provided me with many Life Skills. Here are some highlights:

1. The importance of a budget

2. How to get the most value out of a dollar

3. How to see "Long Term"

4. How to cook

5. How to clean

6. How to bite my tongue

7. How to turn off my own ears

8. How to love a baby

9. She gave me my knowledge of why it is important to breast feed your children

10. If I didn't know it before the importance of self education

11. She is the one who got me hooked on books

12. Salesmanship and customer service

I know there are more but that is quite an impressive list!

Chris no doubt pushed me. She drove me. She was so worried I might fail and she didn't want that to happen on her watch. She wanted to be able to say she had succeeded where my mother had failed.

In my eyes we all fail at some point in our lives; some of us seem to do it more than others. It is our perseverance through our failures that I find the most impressive. Who has never felt like curling up in a ball and dieing? I know I have more than once.

The best way I could describe how Chris felt about me when I

was growing up was this, "She loves to hate me and hates to love me."

Now my only wish for my step-mother is the same wish my

grandma made for me on my 25th birthday; "May you learn how to LIVE before you die."

It took me forever to figure that one out!

I know for all of us in this world. Learning to live before we die will not happen without building a relationship with God. When you take into consideration that Chris helped me with this as a child, I feel I should at least continually try to return the favor. After all, her life depends on it! Everyone's does.

I know that this particular chapter is short and sweet. It also happens to be by far the easiest chapter I have written!

If you are lacking in your faith like my step-mother is, my prayer for you is the same. I simply pray you find yourself on the road to belief.

I leave you with this one simple question, "If there is no creator, if there is no Almighty Father, why does every child on earth seek the approval of their own earthly father?"

I know there are other moms out there reading this who have men in their lives they have conceived children with. Even if those fathers seem to be rotten at their fatherly duties, their children love them and seek their approval regardless. Why?

It is my belief that somewhere deep inside all of us there is an undeniable desire to please Our Heavenly Father. With that being said, I ask you this; "How can you deny God exists?"

The best line I heard about believing in God was last night on my way home from work. I was listening to moody radio and a man was discussing his own sons struggle with faith as he hit the year 19.

While at dinner with his parents, he was asking them how they could believe in a God who allowed young children to die in horrific ways. Without missing a beat his mom said, "Honey don't worry about that. It's natural selection."

You cannot have it both ways. If you feel your heart being torn when you witness the pain of others you are closer to God than you realize. Without God, you would have no heart!

Today, I pray you learn to listen with your heart. I pray you open yourself up to the possibility of God if you are a non-believer.

That is all I have for now. May your day be full of blessings, may you bless a complete stranger,

Wendy, Mom of Many

Chapter Eleven

My Scarlet Letter

The battle between Chris and I had not gone according to plan. The only thing I had accomplished was turning her into a meaner prison guard. Not only had I proven her right by losing my virginity, I had gone one step further and shown her I was capable of doing dark deeds.

That summer was brutal working for Chris. The only highlight to each day was that I got to talk with Debbie, Bill's wife. Chris disliked her as much if not more than she disliked me. It was her pure dislike of the both of us that brought Debbie and I closer.

We had a lot of fun laughing together that summer. She was the only person on earth that could understand the cruelty of Chris completely. She herself had felt the brunt of it personally.

One of my favorite Debbie moments would have to be the day I was in charge of 3 gigantic burn piles. I had wanted to add some highlights to my hair, but doing so was OUT of the question!

Without Chris' knowledge, I had managed to purchase a bottle of this stuff called 'Sun In'. The gist was it worked on heat from the sun.

I had sprayed some into my hair that morning and then I blew my hair dry. I didn't notice any difference. You could say I was not a believer in the whole works on heat thing.

I went out and met my father in the yard. He gave me a quick lesson regarding the fires he was setting and how I was to keep them from growing out of control. I worked those fires for hours. It was a hot day and being in the midst of fire piles made it a

VERY hot day.

I found myself mesmerized by the fires. As I tended to them I realized fire seemed alive to me. The way it moved. The crazy way it jumped. I could even hear it breath.

I'm sure a fire fighter would agree a fire is just shy of a living entity. It's scary amazing.

Anyway, I finally had the three fires down to nothing more than ashes and I was more than ready for some lunch. I went into the office and Debbie exclaimed, "What did you do to your hair?!"

I was a little confused by her reaction to my entrance but. I replied, "I sprayed some 'Sun In' in it this morning but I didn't see a difference."

She couldn't even talk anymore. She managed to say the word mirror as she pointed adamantly to the bathroom. I moved quickly. She looked so shocked, I was a little frightened.

As soon as I saw myself I screamed. My hair literally looked like a fire itself without any blues of course. You could easily say my hair resembled a lion's mane when it came to color!

I got in a little hot water over the change in color. My father wanted me to dye it back to its natural color but Chris allowed it to stay as it was. I think she knew I didn't like how it had turned out!

You could easily make the claim that I developed way too fast as a child. My nick name was weed because I would grow in spurts. By the time I made it to the 6th grade I had the body of a woman.

Personally I have never been comfortable with my chest. It has seemed to be a curse. In the 6th grade I basically went to bed not needing a bra and by morning my mother had to take me shopping for one. It was so bad I couldn't go to school that day without one.

As if that wouldn't be horrible enough had it happened to you, I was called down to the Principal's office that next day. It turns out adults aren't too into instant boobs either! I was told it was unacceptable to stuff one's bra. Let's just say it was one of my first want to ball up and die moments. My nickname was Dolly Parton and Chesty for the remaining year.

I did get a little chunkolicious my freshman year but that weight seemed to drop off over the summer. By the time school was getting ready to start I had slimmed down a lot. I needed new school clothes and Chris was taking me to purchase my school clothes.

My clothing budget was less than my brothers. He earned more because he worked out in the field with my father and always had overtime.

Since I was obviously a 'bad girl' who could not be trusted, Chris had decided my clothes should be very loose as not to outline my body. I had to purchase pants that were a size too big and wear them with a belt. It was so ridiculous that if I took my belt off, some of my pants would fall right off my hips without even being unbuttoned! The irony was not lost on me.

I could have told her I wasn't interested in sex until I was blue in the face. She would not have believed me. I was already labeled a liar so what I had to say held no value.

I hated my wardrobe and I was not thrilled with my life. Around the first month of school being back in session, I made a failed attempt to end my life. All I ended up doing was sleeping off my abundance of swallowed pills.

I had a pretty tough schedule my sophomore year. All college prep classes. My Schedule was so tight we had to bump back taking physical education to my junior year. It simply did not fit in anywhere else. I had no room for a study hall either. Chris was not into idle time at all!

She had signed me up for speech my freshman year because that was the only place it would work in my four-year plan. I was the only freshman in a class of juniors and seniors. I was terrified. The mere thought of standing in front of these strangers and giving a speech had me trembling so bad I can't even explain it. I did not overcome that phobia until 10 years later! Anyway, I decided to withdraw myself out of the class. Back then you just had to get a signature from your parent on a form to withdraw from a class. I forged my father's signature on the withdraw fail form.

When my report card came I was in more trouble than I care to go into. The good news is the school had to take the withdraw failure off my record and that move was enforced by Chris. The school never stood a chance with her arguing against them. My grade point average was unharmed. Yippee.

Looking back, I realize I was not talking to God daily anymore. I knew He was real. That I could not deny. I just no longer believed He was cheering for "Team Wendy".

That year I decided I must have missed something with this whole sex thing. There had to be a reason Chris was so convinced I was into it. I decided the next chance I had to explore this painful activity, I would.

As it happened I had a few band friends that Chris approved of. One night we all went out. We ended up at a house in Carmel and this is so awful to say because I don't even remember my momentary boyfriends name but he was there. We had only hung

59

out a couple times before this night.

Before long, everyone went into separate rooms and I was alone in a bedroom with this boy. He had a condom so no worries about babies.

I was no more thrilled with the result than I was when I had performed the deed with Danny Joe.

Adults, I decided, were crazy. Who in their right mind actually enjoyed this?! The one good thing that had come out of my sleeping with this guy that night, was I received an invite to the Carmel prom. Of course Chris would not let me attend that! Proms produce babies you know!

She informed me I would have time to go to a prom my Junior and Senior year. She explained I was much too young to go to one my sophomore year.

Needless to say, my guy was forced to pick another girl to take to the prom and shock of all shocks I never heard from him again. I would like to say I was sad over that but honestly I was not. I never had deep feelings for him to begin with.

Chris and I had battled numerous times over the year. Once I received an hour long lecture over my opinion of a sitcom.

Another time we battled over me loaning a hair dryer to Tami in the dead of winter. We had two of them. The one I loaned her shut off after 10 minutes and you had to wait for it to cool down

before it would turn back on. Tami had been drying her hair in front of a wood stove so she really needed a hair dryer. She had that hair dryer for 3 weeks when Chris realized it was gone. I was grounded for my deed.

After that incident, I decided Chris was the most selfish person

I'd ever met in my life. One day as summer was fast approaching I asked her, "Would you allow me to get a job working somewhere else?"

By the Grace of God, she conceded. Westfield only had the Dairy Queen back then. I imagine she thought no one would hire me. Unfortunately for her, I was hired right on the spot by Dairy Queen!

I was ecstatic. I had landed my first real job. Chris would no longer be in control of my paychecks. Up until my job at Dairy Queen I had never even seen my paychecks!

The craziest thing Chris ever did to me was attempt to get me fired right before the fourth of July. I showed up for work and my manager, Sheila, pulled me to the side and informed me that my mother had come in earlier and requested that I be fired for my own good.

I was dumbfounded. I didn't even know my mom knew where I was working and for the life of me I had no idea why would she want me fired! My head was spinning. I looked at Shelia and said, "My mom, long brown hair?" and I placed my hand at my waist line.

Shelia looked completely confused and said, "No, shoulder length and auburn."

I was floored. I gasped, "That's not my mom! That's my step-mother!"

Shelia said, "Well, I told her we had no reason to fire you. You're the best worker we have." She informed me that Chris was pretty hot when she left.

The next day I called my mom and told her what was going on

and begged her to let me come live with her for the summer. I don't know why she caved but she did. Chris was not happy but she did not stop me. I don't think she wanted my dad to know the lengths she had gone to in an attempt to run / ruin my life.

I had my mom's car to drive. We had basically the same hours. I would drop her off at work do my shift and go back and wait for her to get off of work and then we'd go home.

I was 16 now and one day, I decided that perhaps I should look up Danny Joe. I did not want to sleep with a bunch of men. It was bad enough that I had already slept with two of them. So much for saving myself and going through life with only one person I chided myself. I figured if I wanted to keep that number from growing it would be in my best interest to track down Danny Joe.

It took me a couple of hours to find that house again. When I did, it was Danny Joe's sister Tracie that I found. She explained that Danny Joe lived with their mom now. She went on to say she hadn't seen him for a couple of months but would she would love to take me over to her mom's apartment.

My heart was pounding so hard on the way over there. I hadn't seen Danny Joe since the day I'd forced him to sleep with me. When we got there he wasn't there yet.

Tracie introduced me to her mom and the front door opened. In came Danny Joe and another boy who turned out to be one of his step-brothers.

Danny Joe was smoking a cigarette. I couldn't believe my eyes. Seeing me standing there, I'm not sure he believed his. He made some snide comment as he walked by me. Something like, "Have you come back around for a boyfriend? That's not how things work. I'm not up for grabs I guess you can have my brother."

I told him, "I don't need your help with finding a boyfriend Danny Joe. I'm quite capable of doing that on my own."

He went on by, plopped down on the couch and his eyes seemed to bore into me. I was doing a pretty good job of glaring right back at him!

I went into the kitchen with Tracie and her mom. She was fixing us lemonade. I stood at the end of the table staring at Danny Joe.

His mom asked how we knew each other. I said, "We met at a Sunday School class four years ago."

His mom seemed surprised. She then informed Tracie that Danny Joe was going to be a dad. I felt the room spin. I don't know how I managed to remain standing.

Danny and his brother headed back out after that. I told Tracie I needed to be going soon myself. I explained I had to work a shift that night and I needed to get ready for work.

Tracie decided she wanted to hang out with her mom. She walked me out to my car and apologized for her brother. She asked me not to be a stranger. I don't even remember what I said. All I remember was I felt like I had been separated from my body. There was no way I could hang around and watch Danny Joe become a father.

That was the last time I ever laid eyes on Danny Joe. It wasn't the last time I thought about him though.

As I drove off I looked up to the heavens and yelled. "Really? Really?"

I was so infuriated at the way my life was turning out. I continued on with my rant to God. "Danny Joe is having a baby? It's not with me! What about this grand plan you had for me? Hugh?

63

Now I have to find someone else? Do you take great joy in this?"

Again I warn you. Anger is not a wise emotion. It clouds your mind and allows you to do things you would not do under normal circumstances. Anger can make you believe things that had someone come right out and stated it you would have not believed.

Satan has a way of whispering to you so softly he can bend your ear and speak to you as if it was you talking to yourself.

Because of this particular power he uses against you, mere anger can turn you into someone you never were. When you feel this emotion taking the wheel in your life, I encourage you to get on your knees and pray.

This is where this chapter ends. May you have a blessed day my friends.

Wendy, Mom of Many

Chapter Twelve

A Shotgun Wedding

That summer I developed a crush on a guy named Jim and another guy named Jeff was interested in me. I have never verified this but I was told by a mutual friend that he was paid $50 to do and say what he did and said to both Jim and me.

I worked drive thru mostly. I was a runner and cashier. It did not matter who I was teamed up with, all of my teams had the best times. Yes, I think this counts as gloating! Anyway, my favorite team was Jimmy and I. There was electricity that flowed between him and I that was undeniable.

I imagine that is why Jeff devised the plan he did. Jeff had this dream of being in a rock and roll band and I always wanted to be a writer. Anyone who knew me for any length of time knew that about me.

Back then I was always writing. Poetry. Short stories. It didn't matter really. At home, both Chris and Dad had made comments about how I was only going to amount to a girl who sat in a corner and wrote. I would do creative writing assignments for fellow classmates just for the challenge it provided me. Sick isn't it? Who desires more homework? Me! That's who.

Anyway, that summer I had offered to write some songs for him and his band. I guess Jeff liked me and wanted to take out the competition because according to our mutual friend Rick he had lied to me about Jimmy after being paid $50 by Jeff to do his evil deed. (This I found out later in life when Rick and I reconnected for a moment a few years down the road)

So the story goes, Jim had kissed me in the cooler the night before. It was amazing. The next day I was informed by Rick that Jim felt like I was throwing myself at him and he really wasn't interested in me. I was told he wished I'd stop flirting with him because he had a girlfriend in Noblesville.

I was devastated. I decided to put up a wall of ice towards Jimmy that he never saw coming. When he went to Rick (our mutual friend) to inquire if he knew what was going on with me, Rick told him that I was not interested in him and felt pressured and wished he'd stop flirting with me.

I was already in my 'no attention given' zone where Jimmy was concerned so, he took Rick's words as truth just as I had.

With Jimmy firmly out of the way, Jeff invited me over to his place to work on some of the lyrics with the band that I still had not met. When I arrived there it was just Jeff. He was 4 years older than me and quite seductive I must admit. While not yet resolved to sleeping with him, I began hanging out with Jeff more and more. I never did meet the rest of his band.

The summer was closing in on the start of school and I had discovered that my step-mother had gone to visit her sister in Kansas and would be gone for two weeks.

It was my belief that she had purposely always gotten in the way of me having a decent relationship with my father. All the way back to my early childhood memories, somewhere between 6 & 8 while visiting on a summer day; I suggested that an ice cream cone sure would help cool things off.

Chris informed my father that I was attempting to wrap him around my little finger and trick him into doing things for me and I must be stopped. This was stated in front of me.

All my life, I truly felt Chris had mandated how close my relationship was with my father. With her gone I thought this would be my last chance to spend some honest quality time with my father without interference.

I discussed this with my mom and I decided going back a week prior to school was what I wanted to do. The same day I went back, Chris came back too. Turns out she had had a falling out with her sister.

Another school in Zionsville offered this 'bring a friend to school day on their first day of school.' A friend of mine, Shelly, went to school there and she had invited me to go to with her for the first day in school.

This was my junior year and the gist was back then when you were in your senior year you could decide where you wanted to go to school if you paid to go outside your zone.

I was such a radical kid back then. I didn't smoke, I didn't do drugs, and I didn't drink. I wasn't even participating in any sexual relationship. I wanted to spend my day off work at a school! Whew! What a wild child I was I thought sarcastically to myself.

When I approached my father with what I intended to do he told me no. Being more open mouthed after a summer with my mother, I questioned his decision. He told me I couldn't go because he did not know this friend.

I pointed out the fact that while he may 'know my friends' he didn't really know them. I suggested that maybe he should just have a little faith in me.

Things got a little hot and he asked me, "Why did you even bother to come back?"

I looked at him and said, "To be honest I was told Chris was in Kansas and I was hoping to have some time with you without her."

He called me a liar.

I said, "You don't (cuss word) believe me, I'll call mom and you can ask her!" and I stomped to the phone.

I grabbed it and marched to the table as he said, "What did you just say to me?"

Being allowed to cuss openly over the summer had just got my rear in hot water. I knew what I'd said but I stated the following, "If you don't believe me, I'll call mom and you can ask her."

It was too late. What happened next was far from pretty. He pushed me into a chair so hard I went head over heals right out of it. Before I had my bearings he was yanking me back onto my feet. I stared intently at the floor. He demanded that I look at him and being me I had to push it. "I refuse to look a maniac in the eyes." I replied.

Things went from bad to worse. It was as he tried pulling me down stairs out of view as well as earshot of my little sister; Chris gave Tommy, my brother, instructions to bar Cady in her room.

I'll never forget how she walked around the corner as calmly as one could and said, "Okay that's enough, let's go downstairs and discuss this."

No sooner than we got down the steps, here came Cady. She was very upset and she demanded to know why my father was beating me up. He assured her he had not been beating me up. He told her that we were only dancing the way that the French people do.

My baby sister is and was no fool. She is now in the profession of helping families with issues.

From that moment I welcomed my destiny and I went to Jeff and gave myself to him. As a matter of fact, I sought out Jeff every morning before school. I was confused though. After two months of this routine, I had not conceived my first child.

I began thinking perhaps my destiny had been cancelled due to my outright spiting God and being angry with him over the last couple of years. I decided perhaps my life was my life after all and I needed a change.

While discussing this with Jeff he informed me that he had connections with someone who could give me a whole new identity. It would cost me $1000 but with that I could buy all I needed to become someone else.

I began budgeting and saving more and figured I'd have that saved up before the end of November. We planned for me to make my final escape come Jan 6th. 1986. You know what they say about the best laid plans.

Prior to Thanksgiving I came down with my annual tonsillitis. These time things had gotten really dangerous. Chris truly believed if my body was forced to fight off the illness without medicine it would become stronger. Unfortunately, I ended up running a dangerously high fever on the third day of being shut in my room.

Chris had come down to check on me, as the story is told by Donna's father who she ran into at Westfield Pharmacy picking up my prescription. He told me she'd said, "Wendy was out of it so, I slid the thermometer into her mouth."

According to the story I sat up and spit the thermometer out and began yelling, "Turn the Page". I had fallen out reading *That*

was Then This is Now, by S.E. Hinton.

My fever in seconds had registered 105 and Chris who weighed maybe 115lbs at the time dragged me up a flight of stairs, got me in the car and drove an hour to her doctor in Tipton with the windows down.

When we got there her doctor was off and I was seen by an alternate. I have never heard a doctor tear into an adult the way he tore into Chris. He threatened not only her but to also have her doctor pulled in front of the medical board if my tonsils were not removed.

That visit, I received a shot of penicillin in my butt and my surgery was scheduled to take place right before Thanksgiving.

This slowed down my ability to stash money a little but it had not stopped me. I had the money required and was now working on funds to carry me until I found a job under my new identity.

Much to my dismay, my father and I ended up in another spat. This time we were in the car and the fight started over my clarinet.

We fought over whether the clarinet was his or mine. It was a pointless argument but I was bound and determined to make a point.

When he went to backhand me due to my smart mouth, I managed to get out of the way. My poor sister ended up getting my punishment for the wise crack.

I was horrified by the chain of events. That night I resolved to leave sooner than planned. I confided this in a notebook that Donna and I passed back and forth between classes.

Somehow my plans to leave were shared with the new school counselor and she called me out of class into her office.

I managed to convince her that I had no plans to leave. I explained to her that this journal was simply my way of venting. I told her I was under an immense amount of stress and had developed a bleeding ulcer. I begged her not to call my parents that day but to allow me to come back to school in the 5th period the next day with my real mother and with her there I would be open to a family meeting. I told her if she called today my parents would keep me from this doctor appointment to have me and my bleeding ulcer looked at.

Lies. Complete lies. If Chris had gotten her hands on my journal, I'd have been hosed. That was the real truth.

I told Donna I was leaving in the morning and she, for some odd reason, decided she wanted to go with me. I told her I'd be going over to the apartments Jeff had lived at and trying to catch a ride to catch another ride to French Lick from there.

I was going to find Jeff and move ahead with my plan of purchasing a new identity. This was December 9th. Almost a month ahead of schedule, but I had more than enough money stashed to jump.

That night I took down my poems and journal that now spanned 3 of the 4 walls in my room from ceiling to 3' above the floor. I left one sign I'd made that stated, "Let he who has not sinned cast the first stone" as well as a poem that started out "Children and Parents, A match made in hell. When I escape, Things will be well."

During the current school year, Chris had ransacked my room often so I put my diary on the wall. I knew she never even looked at what I had put up or we'd have had a talk. She did however stumble upon a decoy letter I'd left in my sock drawer one day. It was a prank letter.

I started it out as if it were meant for a friend and just as it was getting juicy you had to turn the note over. Half way into the second line my sentence changed to; "Hey Chris! I hope you enjoyed this story. I ran out of time to finish!"

I came home to discover my door was off the hinges and I was grounded for a week. Well worth the price is how I viewed my punishment. I was being punished for creative writing in all honesty. She was mad about my pure evilness.

As far as I was concerned, I had proven that she was indeed snooping in my room! She claimed she thought I'd somehow taken some of my sister's socks as the reason for finding the note. That in itself was hilarious to me as I had been doing my own laundry for the last couple of years! She and I both knew Cady's socks were not in my room.

I informed my brother that I was skipping school that next morning. I felt bad about leaving him without telling him what I was really doing, but I couldn't risk him knowing my real plan.

I knew if he knew, they'd know he was holding back information. I reasoned if he knew nothing he'd have nothing to hide. I heard later that he went through a lot of questioning as they were sure he knew something even though he did not.

When I arrived in French Lick I found Jeff's sister Kim but Jeff was not around at the time. He had actually gone back to Westfield for some reason. He showed up on my parent's doorstep looking for me and was informed I had run away. He was honestly surprised at the turn of events as we'd been out of contact since late October. The last he knew the plan was still the plan.

He showed back up in French Lick after I'd been there for 4 days already. The heat was amping in the search for Donna and me. To this day I'm not sure why she came with me, but she did.

Jeff decided it would be best for us to hide out at his parent's farm house for the time being. He was being so sweet and protective over me. He cooked us dinner on the burning stove and I caved in on sleeping with him that night.

The next night, lights panned in the drive and Jeff ushered Donna and I up into the attic. We hid there while the local Sheriff asked some questions and looked around a little. We were not discovered. They had informed Jeff that Donna's boyfriend had been arrested for withholding information and if he saw us we needed to know this. The only way he was going to be released was if we both returned.

After a VERY long discussion, it was decided that we would go back. Jeff did not want to be caught with us so in a gist we had him drop us off and Donna called her dad and he came and agreed to take me to my mother's house.

I don't know why I thought my mother would protect me. I wasn't in her house for 15 minutes when she informed me my father was on his way to come get me. I jumped up grabbed my back pack and ran into my old room. I got in the closet and hid all my writings in the attic. After they were safely stashed I came back out, sat down, and waited for my fate.

My father drove me straight to the police station in Westfield and demanded that justice be served. Running away is against the law. He left me there.

The detective / policeman (back then Westfield had like two police cars) was curious as to how I had escaped. He said, "We had dead end tips from everywhere but seriously, you vanished

73

into thin air. How did you pull it off?"

I was not talking. I knew if they had an inkling of anyone who may have helped us they would be pressing charges on them. I was not going to be a part of punishing those who had only tried

to help me with my scheme. Realizing he was not going to get anywhere he drove me over to Hamilton County Jail.

Even though I was a juvenile they had no room over there so I was being taken to the main jail and was told I would be safely locked in solitary confinement.

I will say this; being booked was an awful experience. I was strip searched, de-liced and completely humiliated.

I've been told by various people in as well as out of the law enforcement field that all of this was necessary. In response to that claim, I state the following: "I don't have to live with their demons. However, I often wonder just how many 'officers of the law' uphold the laws when it comes to themselves. I only know this; they instilled in me a fear of them that runs all the way to my core. I am of the opinion that a couple of the arresting officers inside the jail I was taken to seemed to relish in their 'duties' a bit too much

On my way to being escorted to court, I was informed by the officer taking me that I was only supposed to serve one day in

Hamilton County but since my friend's parents had refused to turn her over, I'd served a day for her as well as a day for myself.

I'm not sure what he had to gain from that comment. Regardless, the elevator opened and I saw my father on a bench and on the other side of the room was Donna with her parents. I was brought over to my father and I sat down on the bench beside him. He

74

said, "Part of me is proud that you have a spine and seem to show no fear here, the other part of me wishes you were more like her." He motioned over to Donna who was currently puking due to the stress of going to court.

When we were called into the room, I asked to be released into my mother's care and was denied. I was being released to my father and step mother. It was now December 20th. By Christmas I knew I was pregnant. I could not believe it. Here I'd tried to push that destiny for two straight months and nothing. Yet, when I ran away, I ended up conceiving.

I decided life was ironic. I hadn't said anything about being pregnant yet. Chris informed me I was being taken to her doctor to be put on birth control. Still I said nothing. When she took me there I was taken back and her doctor began telling me about birth control options. I looked up at him and said, "Shouldn't you perform a pregnancy test before you prescribe me birth control?"

He stared at me and asked if I thought I needed one. I shook my head yes. Sure enough the test was positive and I was taken into another room. He began informing me that it would be in this baby's best interest not to be born. I was shocked. I hit him with two barrels of "How is this upholding the view of 'Saving Lives' and your Hippocratic oath?"

We argued for a moment about the beginning of life and he

finally asked me, "Do you want me to give her the news or will you do it?"

I informed him with an hour ride ahead of me I'd prefer to spill the beans myself.

He told me to get dressed and he'd meet me out in the hall. When I left the room he was standing with Chris and they both turned to look at me. I knew in an instant he had already spilled the beans; So much for doctor patient confidentiality.

A family meeting was called and my fate had been sealed. I would marry Jeff. I felt like I'd been thrown into the dark ages.

Being defiant as hell when it came to Chris and her demands, I did myself no favors. We had had a couple of arguments that I am not proud of. One was when she informed me I was going to have to burn Jeff's letter jacket as part of my punishment.

I told her something like, "If you insist on me having no respect for other's things you may get more than you bargain for. I'll burn down your house before I'll burn his jacket."

Yes. Defiant is a good way to state how I was reacting at this stage of my life. When I was told I had to get married, I flipped out. I begged to be thrown out on my own and disowned.

Chris informed me it was marriage or abortion and seeing how I wasn't 17 yet, they'd march me down the aisle or I could be tied down to a bed and have my baby ripped out of me.

Dead panned I looked at her and said, "You kill my baby, I kill yours." Horrible. I know. I wince at it myself. Like I said, I was defiant to my own detriment.

The day following my threat toward my sister, I was driven to the court house and my father signed the license for me to be married.

I was only allowed two 15 minute calls each day during that time in my life. It had been that way since I moved in. During one of these calls I begged Jeff to find a fake preacher. I told him, "My parents aren't going to check the credentials of the person performing the ceremony. I will live with you but please understand I don't want to marry you. I am not ready to be married at all."

I don't know why Jeff thought it would be in his best interest to force me to say vows I didn't long to say but he did. Knowing in my heart that once married, divorce was frowned down upon, I felt like I was in the midst of a nightmare.

I decided that this must be the beginning of my new life and I cried my way down the aisle and faced my fate like the trooper I had become!

This has been a long chapter I know. As you have read, I was not the smartest when it came to dealing with how my parents felt about me and how I was living my life. Unwise decision after unwise decision without input from God had taken me right from the frying pan to the skillet so to say.

In the years to come you will witness again and again how far one can go on the road to hell. At various times in my life, you'd almost believe I was on a race to see who could get there first!

Today I pray that before you react to some event in your life, you take the time to pray on it. Sit still for a moment or two. Blessings to all who try,

Wendy, Mom of Many

You Are Worthy Too

Marriage Motherhood and My Moral Meltdown

By Wendy Glidden

Copyright 2014 Wendy Glidden

Dear Reader,

First I want to take this opportunity to thank you for purchasing the second volume in my life series. Publishing books has been a life long dream. I must admit, I never thought it would be myself that I would be writing about.

In my first Dear Reader letter, I told you a little about myself. This time I thought it would be fun to share a poem I wrote recently. I hope you enjoy it!

I have so much to be joyous about.
It makes me laugh and sing and shout!
Life is abundant, I am free
Curious as to how I came to be?

I am not here to brag or boast
It's The Good News I love to share the most.
God called me out over a year ago
It's in sharing our story others will come to know

God is FAITHFUL, good and true
He sent His son to save me and you!

The Good News is the Best News you will ever hear
If you're not deaf, you'll give a mighty cheer
If you are blind, you will sadly only sneer
But those that are able to see will be free from fear!

So if today you have found that you are at the end of yourself
I am here to share a story of hope and faith I pray it helps
The roads I have traveled have at times been dark and long
Throughout my life chapters I reveal how I've remained strong

I've been told by others that they have walked a similar street

A cool part of my life today would be the others I meet
I am here show you God's mercy, grace and glory
They are intertwined throughout my life story.

I hope through sharing my life with you,
Seeking the Lord becomes something you naturally do
For when you seek, you will discover an abundance that never
ends
P.S. I'm always looking for fellow sisters and brothers for friends

Love, Wendy Glidden

Chapter 1

How I Became a High School Drop Out

Just prior to me being married off after discovering I was pregnant, I was sentenced into my father's custody. I was placed on probation and ordered to obtain counseling. My counselor was a man who had adopted quite a few foster children. I think he had like seven.

Somewhere in our first conversation I had mentioned I loved to write. He asked if I would be willing to share some of my stuff with him. I honestly liked the guy so I said I would.

When we met the second time I gave him some of my poems. He read the first few and looked at me for a moment. Then he said something like this; Wendy, I don't have anything to teach you. I don't think you are messed up at all. You understand more about life than I think your parents give you credit for. I will tell your probation officer that as well. From now on, I want you to take the $30 you are supposed to give me and spend this time and money on yourself.

I can't remember if he knew I was being forced to get married or not. I think he did. At the time I don't think either of us realized the date was going to be set so quickly.

While not loving the fact that I had to be married off; while not thrilled with the fact that I had no voice in the decision, somewhere inside of me was the belief that once married, that was your chosen partner for life. I was determined to make this work. I reasoned anything had to be better than being under Chris' rule.

Jeff and I got married on Feb 11th, 1986.

You may be asking yourself; why did she need to get married so fast?

I truly don't know the answer to that. I have run some possible reasons through my head over the years. These are what I came up with:

1. The date had to be set so soon to ensure I would get married. (If I was allowed to pick a time, say after March 6th, I would be 17 years old and the state law regarding parents having the right to insist upon their child having an abortion would no longer apply to me. In other words; I would be able to keep my baby and not have to get married.)

2. Because of my hateful and insane responses to the demands Chris had made on me, they wanted me out of the house as soon as possible. By insisting on me marrying Jeff they would no longer be responsible for me as far as the courts were concerned.

3. To make it look like I WANTED to get married and was not getting married because I was pregnant.

4. Your guess is just as good as mine.

Any way you slice it, in the end I was married right before my 17th birthday.

So, here I was wed to a guy that I had begged not to marry me. I told myself, 'he must think I'm an awesome catch to insist upon marrying me. He surely must love me to feel that strongly when it came to being a family.

I reassured myself that he was originally going to help me gain my freedom. Surely he wanted to marry me not to trap me but to show me how much he wanted to be a good father to this baby.

I knew I was pregnant with a girl. That was what I had been told. I was going to have many children and the first one was going to be a girl. Since I knew that she was going to be a she, I called her baby girl until I picked out her name. I decided upon Cassandra

for her first name. It took me a little longer to pick out her middle name. I decided upon Nicole while living with Jeff's family.

I wanted a name that would provide her with options regarding what name she wanted to be called by her friends. I felt this combination sounded good together and the two names had a lot of nick names that she could also pick from.

I thought that I would continue going to high school for the remainder of my junior year. After all, Dr. Murry, the principal of Westfield High School had written the state board of education requesting I receive an exception on how many semesters I needed to get my diploma and I had been granted that exception!

I had more than enough credits to qualify for my diploma already. I only needed to drop an English class and take Psychology in its place. I met all other qualifications. My grades were excellent and my school record was impressive all the way back to the 7th grade.

Dr. Murry gave me the good news that I had been granted the exception at the same time he told me I could not continue my education at Westfield Washington High School.

I was so confused. He told me he would be happy to look the other way when it came to the fact that I was living in Noblesville, but that my step mother was forcing the issue.

You see, after I was married to Jeff, I had moved into the apartment he had found us in Noblesville. We were 7 miles to the east of Westfield. Because I was only a junior at the time, I did not retain the right to go to school where I wanted to. Somehow Chris Glidden knew that. She had insisted that I not be allowed to attend High School at Westfield.

Dr. Murry, the principal of our High School, truly felt bad. He told me something close to this as he gave me my student file; normally this would just be transferred from school to school but you are now considered an adult and there is no cause for me not to give it to you. I think you need to see your file and all that is in it for yourself. You will need it to enroll yourself in Noblesville. You're still in Hamilton County. Our credit system is the same so you will still be allowed to graduate at the end of this school year. You'll just be graduating from Noblesville High School instead of here.

He wished me luck and walked me out of his office. I knew he felt bad about what was happening. Me, I was in a daze as I left the school grounds.

"Why does she hate me so much? What did I ever do to her?" I wondered.

The next day some of Jeff's friends who were still in High School and who were actually attending Noblesville High School arrived in the morning as agreed to pick me up. I had my marriage license and my high school record in hand. I went into the office and asked for the forms to enroll myself.

At the time, many of the counselors in this school were also probation officers. I had been assigned one of them because I was on probation.

Our first meeting did not go well. She sat across from me and reviewed my file. She closed it as she tossed my letter from the State Department of Education at me and said, "This may have flown at your other school but you are not going to be graduating at the end of the school year from here. A lot of your credits don't count."

If I had been allowed to take any fluff classes at all, I could have understood that. The closest I had come to a fluff class in high school would have been typing! I was shocked at what she was telling me.

She went on to tell me this, "The only way I see you graduating ahead of your class is if you take a couple of summer courses and the first semester of your senior year."

"My baby is due in September!" I balked. "I can't possibly do that."

She informed me that was not her problem. If I thought I was going to get rewarded for setting a bad example to fellow students I was wrong.

Perplexed but wanting to graduate, I bit my tongue. I did request that she be kind enough to keep the married and pregnant thing on the down low. I told her I didn't want my teachers to judge me or treat me differently because of it. She claimed she could do that much for me.

It was on my way to 5th period that day that I came up behind her as she was informing my next teacher all about me. What she had to say about me could be categorized as sheer gossip. I was angry to say the least. I did not care for Noblesville High School one bit.

I was worried how I was going to manage to graduate on time now. I was thinking about possible ways that might work. Maybe I could go to summer school and then take classes in the second semester of High School instead of the first semester. Maybe I could even go half days. Then I wondered; who would baby-sit for me while I went to school?

I did not sit down and talk to God at this time of my life. I felt I had been abandoned by Him. I truly believed there was no reason for me to turn to Him. I no longer believed I was worthy of conversation.

As much as I hated going to classes at Noblesville High School, I went. A degree was important to me. Just as I had resolved myself to finishing out the school year, Jeff came home with the bad news. Not only had he lost his part time job that night, he had been fired that day from his full time job that same morning.

He informed me we were moving to French Lick, Indiana. He explained that we would be moving in with his parents. I felt like I was living in the midst of a nightmare. I went to school and withdrew myself the next day. I asked about the requirements that a person needed to be able to take the GED exam. The lady in the office informed me that I would need to be out of school for one year and I would have to be 17 years old.

No problem I thought! I could take the exam one month prior to my class graduating with real high school diplomas!

I am out of time and must end here. I hope you are enjoying my story and can relate to my life in some way.

It is my hope that you see me to the end. It does have a happy ending. Perhaps I should say middle as I am not done living quite yet!

Today I pray for all high school drop outs. I pray for all teen moms. I pray for all who are in a relationship that they wish they were not in. I pray for all who are in the midst of a struggle of any kind. May you find your strength in God much earlier in life than I did. In Jesus name I pray. Amen.

Wendy, Mom of Many

Chapter 2

In the Nick of Time

It was around the end of April, 1986 when Jeff and I packed up all our belongings and loaded everything into his father's car and headed to French Lick Indiana.

To say I was nervous would be an understatement. I had never met Jeff's parents. I truly had no idea what to expect.

To this day when I think of Charlie, Jeff's dad, I can't help but smile. He was always nice to me. Charlie had his own hang-ups like we all do but I loved him for who he was. He never wronged me. He had a sense of humor. All in all he was a great guy.

We didn't have a lot of belongings so packing up into Charlie's car didn't really take that long. Once we were loaded up we hit the road. I had run away to French Lick so I knew we had a three-hour drive ahead of us. For the life of me I have no idea what all we talked about for the three hours. All I remember was how happy Charlie was with his new sayings for me. One of them was; Wendy Weaver wobbles but she won't fall down. The other one was; Wimpy, wimpy, wimpy, hefty, hefty, hefty. Both of these stemmed from commercials.

When we arrived we were shown our room. We were given the enclosed front porch for our own room. It was the length of the front of the home. It didn't take long for us to unpack and get settled.

Brenda, Jeff's mom, was not near as open and friendly as Jeff's dad. Looking back, I understand. Jeff was her only son. I'm not 100% positive she even knew we were getting married or if she was even invited. I do know this; she resented me for 'tricking' her son into marrying me! Oh the irony of it all does not escape me.

My first real conversation with Brenda was basically her informing me that I would most likely not carry this child to full term. According to her, it was kind of a family curse. As if that was not reassuring enough, she went on to ask me if I realized I might have a downs syndrome child should I somehow manage to not miscarry. She had some articles on my odds all prepared for me.

You could color me stunned. I had taken advanced biology in high school. I honestly knew more than I cared to know when it came to birth defects and crib death!

I took the articles she gave me and I went into our room. I confided in Jeff that night that I felt his mom did not like me because she thought I'd trapped him into marrying me. I asked if he would be so kind as to tell her the truth concerning that. I'm not sure if she knows to this day that it was Jeff that trapped me! I do know that he confided this truth to our 2nd child just this last year! Progress. You just never know when it will happen.

Brenda and I hit heads over applying for welfare and after that she thought of me as a spoiled brat. I know this because that is what she called me to my face.

I bit my tongue. She could not have been further from the truth. I asked her why we should go on welfare when Jeff had no issues keeping him from getting a job.

She told me that jobs were hard to come by so I went out and got one!

I had only been working for three weeks when my boss informed me that due to my condition they were going to have to let me go. I was surprised but could do nothing about it.

Living with Jeff's parents was stressful on me. It didn't make matters any better that Jeff had an older sister who was not a fan of mine.

When I had run away, his youngest sister and I had quickly become friends. I think it was our fourth night that this older sister and her boyfriend were arguing and they had taken the time to put their three children outside of the trailer during the fight. Mindy, the younger sister that had become friends with Donna and I, was informed that the children were outside and the youngest one was supposedly in nothing more than a diaper. The three of us went and scooped the children up and took them while her sister and boyfriend could be heard still fighting inside. The mother of these three did not even come looking for her children until the next day!

I don't know how I became her target but I did. She told awful lies about me. She claimed I'd said things I would not have said. The best part of all of that was Jeff questioning me about it all.

I told him, "If you don't trust me, there is really no point in continuing this marriage."

Out of sheer desperation, I contacted my father and explained to him that I was leaving French Lick with or without his help.

He listened to me. I think perhaps for the first time in his life. Regardless, he ended up offering a job to Jeff and I arranged for him to pick me up the next day.

When Jeff and I had time to talk that night, I informed him that I was going back to Westfield. I told him he had a job if he wanted it. He told me he was not going to work for my father. To which I replied, "I am leaving tomorrow. You can come with me or you can stay here. If you are not at Glidden Fence come Monday, I'm filing for divorce."

To say; the tension was in the air, would be an understatement! The next day my father showed up and I threw what few items I had to my name in the back of the truck and we drove away. Jeff did not join us that day. It was just my father and me.

When we got back to Westfield, my father took me to the office. He informed me that I had 3 hours to use the phone and find a place to stay.

"I can't help you with a place to live." he informed me. "Offering Jeff a job and coming to get you is all I am able to do."

I understood. The last time I had seen Chris, she'd informed me not to set so much as a foot on her front porch.

My first call that day was to my mom. She too said she could not help me with a place to live. She had a roommate at the time and said she could not take me in.

I cannot tell you how lost I felt. I was unable to reach my grandma. She was already in Michigan at her summer home.

I don't know what made me think of Julie Martin, a friend from high school, but I did. I called her. I explained my situation and amazingly her parents opened their home up to me. Julie's mom was one of the kindest souls I have ever had the pleasure to know.

Surprisingly enough, Jeff showed up Monday morning at Glidden Fence. He had moved in with his best man's parents in Noblesville. He made a million promises to me at the time. I figured if he was going to commit himself to being a good providing husband who was I to stop him?

I was 7 months pregnant when Jeff found us a place to rent. We moved in the second week of July.

I have an uncle who is only 7 months older than me. On his 18th birthday, while rebelling against my grandma, Jeff had agreed to let my uncle who is also named Jeff move in with us.

We had not been in this place for a whole month when our landlord informed us that he had sold the house and we would have to evacuate the premises by September 1st! Our baby was due September 14th!

Amazingly enough we did find a one-bedroom apartment to move into. My uncle had already found a new girlfriend and he moved in with her.

September 14th came and I thought I was going into labor that night. My mom came over as she was my ride to the hospital but it turned out I was only having Braxton Hicks contractions. My mom had always told me her labor didn't hurt that bad so I really had no clue as to what to expect.

Seven days later, I awoke to a sharp pain followed by another uncomfortable pain 4 minutes later. I thought I was having some type of indigestion or something. Then another one came 3 minutes later followed by another one 3 minutes later.

I woke Jeff up and said, "I think I'm really in labor this time! I'm having pain every 3 minutes!" We had been told with your first baby your contractions start 10 to 15 minutes apart. He started timing me himself. I think he thought I was not doing it right. I called my mom. I knew we didn't have time to mess around. She lived 45 minutes away and we had a 45-minute drive to the hospital!

Jeff confirmed that my contractions were only 3 minutes apart and my mom said she was heading out the door. 11 contractions later, they began coming every 2 minutes. By this time a friend of Jeff's named Jeremy had stopped by. I think he was more panicked than Jeff or I! By the time my mother showed up, he was suggesting we call for an ambulance!

Between contractions I climbed down the flight of stairs and got in the back of my mom's car. Jeff got in the front seat. Don't think he wouldn't have let me sit up front, he would have. I needed to lie down or so I thought. I think I sat up and laid down a few hundred times finding comfort in no position.

When we arrived at the hospital my contractions were a minute apart. They rushed me into an exam room and the ER doctor checked me. I was dilated to 9cm and they rushed me to a delivery room.

I had been going to the St. Vincent Clinic for all my care. Being a clinic patient on a sliding scale meant that you were being seen by mostly med students.

I had agreed to be a ginny pig for an epidural. They called in the med student and had me roll on my side. He was quick. I never felt a thing. Might be because I was in so much pain at the time! They rolled me on my back and the entire room was in motion.

The doctor on call was still trying to get situated when the next contraction hit. I bore down and basically roared from somewhere deep inside. I remember him saying, "I'm not ready yet, don't push, pant pant blow."

Anyone who has gone through the pain of child birth knows when you get to this point it is all natural. There is no holding back! When my next contraction hit I yelled, "You pant pant blow, I'm pushing!" and whoosh, Cassandra Nicole entered the world.

From start to finish I was in labor with my first child for a whopping 2 hours and 15 minutes!

I think the funniest thing about my first time giving birth was this; 10 minutes after Cassy entered the world, my entire lower body went completely numb! I had not one bit of pain for the next few hours!!

Being as young as I was, and having a mom and dad as young as they were, you could say my hospital room was packed. The nurse came in to inform everyone in the room if they weren't grandparents or sisters and brothers they had to leave the room. No one left!

Slowly the room emptied out as each grandparent and great grandparent was done admiring her. When my step mother bent down to say good bye she informed me she thought is was total crap that I didn't suffer enough during childbirth. She had been in labor for 24 hours with my sister. I would like to say I was shocked by her statement. If I did, I would be lying.

This is a good place close this chapter. I'm sure I've mentioned it once or twice but this decade of my life spiraled further and further down. The longer I remained disappointed and let down by God, the more alone I felt. Of course if you knew me back then, I'm not sure you would have picked up on that. I had never been one to cry on someone else's shoulders! I have friends that claim I'm strong. I tell them, "Girl, I'm no different than you. I cry and wail like the best of them!"

I hope to be back to write a few more chapters. I just don't know their titles yet. I have been given one but it is up the road a bit. I've got approximately 3 years to cover before I get to it. I am Praying for guidance as I continue.

Wendy, Mom of Many

Chapter 3

How I Ended up Pregnant with My 2nd Child

I never had any counseling over the incident that happened that summer day when I was 14.

If you have been molested in any way and you think that you can shove it back into the recesses of your mind and keep it locked safely away, I am here to say, "It did not work for me."

As I mentioned in my first book, one of the gifts Chris gave me was the knowledge regarding breast feeding your children. I had every intention of breast feeding Cassandra until she turned 1. What I didn't count on was falling prey to a form of depression the longer I breast fed her.

I was enrolled in a program for Woman, Infants and Children when I was pregnant with Cassy. When I went in for my appointment a few weeks after her birth, they checked our Iron levels. The results were not good.

The nurse explained to me that I was not doing Cassy a lot of good by breast feeding her because my iron count was too low. She insisted that I change Cassandra over to formula.

I didn't really know until I quit breast feeding that I had been in some kind of funk but I snapped out of it once I stopped breastfeeding. Almost overnight I went from depression right into a cleaning maniac.

There was a loft above our place and it had obviously not been touched for years. There was a broken window so birds had been in and out of it. It needed to be cleaned!

Jeff's friend Jeremy had been crashing on our couch. I had him help me carry something down and when he took a look at the space, he thought it would be perfect. We agreed with a little elbow grease it would be good. He helped me attack that room and in one weekend we had it blinging! He moved a bed up there along with his stuff. It was a win win.

Everything was great until the land lord stopped by. She had seen the fan in the upstairs window and insisted that we could not use the space even though it was on our side.

Before I even knew what was going on, she and Jeremy were arguing about it. Needless to say, she informed me she was evicting Jeff and me over the incident. She must have gone to the court house that day. We were served papers the next day. I was dumbfounded.

I think Jeff must have talked to my father about the incident. I'm not really sure how he got Chris to agree to it though. Somehow, it had been decided that we were moving in with Chris and my dad for three months so that they could help us save our money so that we could build a nest egg.

To say that it was weird to live under my parent's rule while married would be an understatement. Jeff and I found a new place and signed a lease within 3 months as planned.

We had $1000 nest egg in the bank when we moved into our new place. I thought we were really going to be okay. In less than 3 days of opening that account our balance went from $1000 down to less than $50! As it turned out, Jeff owed some bank money from before we were married. He had been served a judgment on the defaulted loan and when we put the money in our bank account, they froze the funds and took them. I was sick over it.

Our apartment was right in the middle of town. A new Gas

America had just been built and it was 2 blocks down the road. On a whim I went and applied for a job. They were looking for someone to fill the grave yard shift.

I wanted that job so badly. Jeff only gave me $40.00 a week for groceries and household needs. Even back then it was not a lot! I needed an income of my own to fill in the gap. Grave yard would work perfectly. I reasoned this because Jeff would have Cassy while she slept at night so he didn't really have to take care of her and since he was there with her, I didn't have to spend money on a sitter.

Next I found out about where I could take my GED. I signed up Jeff and me both for GED classes. I told him that he and I were both going to go to class and take this test. My mother had already agreed to come up and sit with Cassy while we attended class.

I am happy to say even with taking my test going on two days of no sleep I was 1-point shy of a full paid state college scholarship! I did not even know at the time that you could get a scholarship on a GED diploma.

My teacher was so excited when she told me how close I was to earning it. She said I could retake the test.

I told her I did not have another $16 at the time to take the test again.

She told me not to worry; I could simply retake the history exam and pay only $4.00!

I laughed and told her I would think about it. Honestly I didn't believe I had the capability to go to college.

Jeff passed his test as well. To this day he will happily admit he is thankful I pushed him to pursue his degree.

We were young when we got married and to say we had a great foundation would be a lie.

By March we had taken on roommates to help with the rent so we really had no time alone together. I think looking back it was the beginning of the end.

We were getting to a point where I was being informed that I had wifely duties and he was not going to go without. Just trust me when I say; when it becomes a 'duty', you better do something about it.

I was on the pill and had been since my last checkup. The last thing I wanted was another baby. I was already thinking I needed to get out of this marriage.

It's funny how abuse starts. It's not like one day they walk up and punch you. An abusive man has to beat you down before he beats you up the first time.

You could easily say Jeff and I were in the beat you down stage of our relationship, so I left him and moved in with my mother near the end of June, 1987.

I was still working grave yard at Gas America at this time. It was in May that I suddenly started having problems with my cycle. Planned Parenthood thought perhaps my body had overcome the pill and I needed a stronger version so they changed my prescription. The next month I had the same problem, so they changed my pill again. The next month I blacked out at work from excessive bleeding and they decided perhaps I needed to have an exam to see if they could spot any cause.

So, there I was on the exam table wondering what on earth was wrong with me. I will never forget the gasp the Doctor made.Do you know how many thoughts can flash across a person's brain in a single moment? I promise quite a few: Cancer, a tumor, had to be something bad. My mind was racing. Nothing I had thought of had prepared me for her next words, "Oh my! You're pregnant!"

Have you ever had your world shatter in a single second? I was astonished by her words. What she said next was even more shocking.

"You're not a little pregnant. If I had to guess, I would say you are almost 20 weeks pregnant. Have you not felt the baby move?"

I was speechless for a moment. Still stunned I managed to say, "No. I haven't."

She then told me, "Well, I'm no expert, but that is my best guess by the size of your uterus."

She went on to make the comment that I had a backward uterus. She mentioned something about the position of my cervix. I felt like I was drifting a million miles away.

I think I mumbled something like; "Is that a bad thing?"

She replied nonchalantly, "No, it's just they used to think girls born with a backward uterus had a more difficult time conceiving a child. You have proven that is not the case!"

I asked her if she thought anything might be wrong with my baby since I'd been on the pill this entire pregnancy.

As far as she knew there just wasn't any available information on that.

She left the room and I numbly dressed myself. I felt like I was disconnected from reality. Surely this was not really happening I told myself. Pregnant? I was in an absolute fog.

Today I pray for all women who find themselves unexpectedly pregnant and are not immediately joyous over their blessing. I have stood in your shoes way too many times. May God fill you with peace and send His servants your way at once. In Jesus name I pray. Amen

Wendy, Mom of Many

Chapter 4

It's a Boy!

I left Planned Parenthood in a daze. To say I was thrilled with my news would be a lie. Here I was again, on the edge of living my own life, on my own terms, only to become pregnant with another baby.

I knew I would have to tell Jeff. I was sick over my situation. I headed back to my mother's house because at that time that was where I was currently staying.

I gave my mom the news. She was as surprised as me. "You haven't felt the baby move?" she asked.

"No. Not yet." I muttered.

I was concerned about what taking the pill day after day might have done to this baby. There was simply no data. It made sense. After all, who takes the pill day after day while being pregnant? I'll tell you who: a girl who has no idea she is pregnant. That's who!

I did not know you could have breakthroughs while carrying a baby. I had never once thought I might be pregnant. I was so numb that first day.

My mom informed me there were two states that offered abortions beyond 12 weeks. She wanted me to know she would never judge me if I decided to take a look into it. I couldn't.

Days later I felt the baby move. I was worried about things like; would the baby have any birth defects? I also wondered if the pill would somehow affect this child's reproductive organs. There were so many unknowns.

The only thing I did know for certain was I had to let Jeff know.

He came by to pick me up so we could talk privately. He told me he was sure this baby was a boy. He asked me to give him another chance. He apologized for his temper. He promised me that it was all a mistake.

I honestly didn't feel like I really had a choice in the matter. Leaving Jeff and raising one child on my own was going to be tough enough. Two would be that much harder. I felt that I was trapped in a hopeless situation. I caved to his plea.

Jeff promised to find us a place immediately and he did. We moved into a one room efficiency apartment. We lived there until October or November. I am not sure which month it was. I am sure of this; I moved in on opening weekend for deer hunting.

My Aunt Janet helped me move because Jeff was off hunting. She was still getting around at the time without a wheel chair. Looking back, I am impressed at how much she was able to due at the time. She was always an inspiration to me.

I never saw a doctor other than the one at Planned Parenthood that had told me I was pregnant, so I had only a good guess as to when I might be due.

I had originally thought I could go back to St. Vincent's OBGYN Clinic since that was where I had gone with Cassandra. However, Jeff was making a little more money and costs had gone up slightly since her birth. Our total cost for all care and delivery was going to be $800.

We did not qualify for a payment plan. Just as it was with Cassandra, I was already around 6 months along when I was in a place where I could seek care. The clinic required you to be paid in full by your 7th month. We simply did not have the full amount!

We also made a hair too much to qualify for Medicaid. Jeff went to work and asked for a loan. Unfortunately for me, Chris decided we needed to learn a lesson when it came to responsibility. She simply could not allow for me to get another easy ride. She believed if I was not held accountable for my reckless behavior when it came to conceiving children, I would continue to have them. She put her foot down. There was no way they were going to bail me out financially again and again.

I never found a doctor. Luckily, Jerry's girlfriend was going to nursing school at the time and she had a stethoscope. She was able to let me hear the baby's heartbeat.

It was at my brother's birthday party on January 16th, 1988, around 7:30 PM, when the first pain hit me.

Uncomfortable is as good a description as any. After about the 6th one I told Jeff I thought my labor had started. We decided that we should head to my mom's house. The plan was for her to keep Cassy when I went into labor.

My father lived in Westfield and my mom was still in the same house she had lived in since I was in the 3rd grade. In other words, we had a 30-minute drive ahead of us and then we needed to turn around and drive another 30 to 40 minutes to the hospital.

Just like with Cassy, my labor pains started four to five minutes apart. I wasn't sure of the exact timing as I'd sat at Chris and dads for the first few labor pains without a clock to look at.

We arrived at Riverview Hospital in the ER entrance. Dr. Beaver was the doctor on call. I remember his name because I found it funny that his name rhymed with Weaver.

William did not come as easily as Cassandra. I was offered pain medication but I refused to take any. I knew we simply could not afford it.

I had pushed several times with William and I was getting nowhere. I felt like someone was ripping my spine out of my body.

My mom was hoping this baby would arrive before midnight so that he'd be born on my brother's birthday. That did not happen. I guess William wanted his own day because he waited until after midnight to make his appearance.

I was beginning to think I'd never push him out when Jeff leaned down to me and said, "Wendy, the doctor is going to use those salad spoons if you don't push this baby out this time!"

When the next contraction hit I pushed with everything I had and whoosh out came the baby. There was no stopping between head and shoulders. I don't know why the thought of salad spoons terrified me to such a degree but it did.

"It's a boy! I told you! It's a boy!" Jeff exclaimed. He even kissed me.

I'm not sure I ever heard Jeff so elated. I was just thrilled to have the birth behind me. He looked perfect. He was a healthy 9lbs 6oz. baby boy. He had the straightest long nose I'd ever seen on a baby but nothing looked out of place. I was relieved to say the least.

Today I pray for all women who are pregnant and unsure of the health of their unborn child. I have had the pleasure of meeting countless children that others would consider unfortunate. Today

I see them as blessed. Should you find yourself blessed with a child that is special in some way, may you know that you will be blessed beyond belief by their love alone. In Jesus name I pray. Amen.

Wendy, Mom of Many

Chapter 5

Staring Down the Barrel of a Shotgun!

Before I start on this journey, and it is longer than I remembered; Harder in many ways; for it goes on much further beyond this tiny chapter, I ask you not to feel sorry for me.

This is for those of you who are here, on this same turn in the road, I'm here to let you know a lot of us have been here, way too many of us. I'm coming back to help.

I don't know completely all the ways God is going to use me, but I'm humbled to be His vessel.

If you are in a situation of utter hopelessness, please, reach out to someone. If you feel you have no one, reach out to me. I make a great friend (((hugs))).

I am not going to go into great detail on my abuse. Jeff never considered what he did to me as abuse for he never outright punched me.

With that being said, I'm a planner. I knew the odds were good that an abusive person would remain an abusive person.

So, for fun, I would run this emergency drill.

I think I had myself convinced it was really in case our house caught on fire. Regardless, I practiced fleeing my home with two children in hand.

I kept a set of keys by the back door. I would start the drill from my bed which was in the back section of the living room. From there I ran down the hallway into the first bedroom. I would scoop up Billy and then I would dash into the back bedroom and grab Cassandra. Next I would grab my keys, go out the back door and race to the car. I'd put Cassy in first and tell her to get in the back seat. Then I'd get in the car, lock the doors, put Billy in his pumpkin seat, put the key in the ignition and fire the car up.

My heart is racing as I recall this myself in more detail. Obviously, one running from a fire only would not have to practice a fire drill to this extent. I find it funny how we trick ourselves into not seeing fully what is going on in our world as it is going on.

I don't know if Jeff and I could have made it with a ton of counseling as well as a healthy relationship with God. I never wanted to marry him to begin with. When you couple that with everything else, we had a rather large hurdle to overcome.

Perhaps the knowledge that I honestly hadn't wanted to marry him to begin with was what drove him to behave the way he did. I don't know the cause but I have a hunch that the true whisperer of lies was behind all of it.

Regardless of what the driving force was, one night his mother planted a fatal seed into Jeff's mind. I think it was around May or June because there was no snow on the ground and it was warm enough that having no shoes on didn't bother me.

Jeff had been gone all evening. He was in town visiting his mom. I'm not sure if his parents were living in Noblesville yet or if his mom was still in the process of looking for a place. He still was not home by 9 P.M. and I had gone to bed. I am not sure when he came home. I just know I went from a dead sleep to being ripped out of bed by my hair. I hit the floor and somehow managed to come up on my feet. I don't think I fully knew it was Jeff attacking me right away. You can't imagine the heart explosion that causes someone.

Somehow I managed to get my bearings. I realized it was Jeff. He was yelling at me. He was calling me awful names and insinuating that William was not his child.

His mother and her friend had been showing him baby pictures of a childhood friend of his. They thought this guy was William's father.

They had informed Jeff that because William's eyes were hazel instead of brown, Jeff couldn't be the father. They convinced him that I must have slept with this other guy.

Jeff was out of his mind furious. He actually attempted to kick me. He would have nailed me full force in the stomach had I not evaded the blow.

His foot went into our stereo system. An album in the top shattered upon impact.

He was momentarily stuck. I didn't hesitate. I ran down the hall way and grabbed William. Then I rushed to the next room. I scooped Cassandra up out of bed like a pro. I snatched the keys, went out the back door, and raced down to the car. I opened the door for Cassy and she hopped in the back just like we had practiced. I sat in the car, locked the doors and put William in his pumpkin seat. I snapped the harness into its slot, put the key in the ignition, and started the car. When I looked up, I found myself staring into the barrel of a shotgun.

Jeff was 8 feet in front of my car with his shotgun drawn.My breath caught. I knew Jeff could be dangerous, but I had no idea until that moment how far he was willing to go.

I dropped my shifter into 2nd gear and hit the gas. Yanking the steering wheel to the left; I spun my tires kicking out gravel like none other. As far as I was concerned it was him or me. I never heard a shot and I didn't feel a thud. I raced down the road without a clue as to where I could or should go. I didn't stop until I was at the stop sign by US 31. I put the car in neutral pulled my emergency brake and sat shaking like a leaf. I was alive. It was all I could think.

From the back seat Cassy asked, "Mommy are you okay?"

I somehow managed to get a grip. I put on a fake smile glanced at her in the rearview mirror and lied. I told her everything was fine.

I had no idea what time it was other than it was very very late or very very early. I drove to the closest house I could think of; my friend Aretha's house from high school. She was still living at home. She answered the door and let me in. I told her what had happened and I think I stayed there until daylight.

I really can't recall much more about that day. I don't think it matters a lot.

I would like to say that I never spent another moment with Jeff after this incident. Sadly, that is not the case.

Today I pray for all those who are in an abusive relationship. May you have faith in Our Father and walk out that door knowing that you will be better off. May you open yourself up to strangers who long to help you. I pray you step out in absolute faith knowing God will always take care of you. I pray you recognize you do not deserve to be treated like this. I pray you are able to open your eyes to the truth. In Jesus name I pray. Amen. Wendy, Mom of Many

Chapter 6

How I Became a Single Mother

I did not call the police. I never reported the incident. I had nowhere to go so I went back.

The entire next year is kind of a blackout for me. I thought perhaps if I reflected on it I could remember it all better. This did not prove to be the case. I have remembered things down the road but this year must have been dark as night, for the details are dim.

It was shortly after that attack when I decided I needed to get myself to a place where I was not dependent upon another person for anything.

I went into town and applied for my old job at Dairy Queen. I was hired on the spot and within a very short time, I was promoted to Breakfast manager. The new position came with a raise!

Seeds when planted will often grow. This is the case with the seed that Jeff's mom had planted. Even though I had shown him scientifically that we could have children with green, hazel or blue eyes because we both had those recessive genes, he still had doubts about my faithfulness.

Within a few months of the initial attack, Jeff was told that I had been seen in our car with another guy driving through Noblesville. When he came to me with this information, I was dumbfounded. I told him it was all lies and nonsense. I offered to take him to work with me so that I could show him my time card.

I don't know why he refused to take a look. He was convinced that somehow I could get around a time card since I was a manager.

Without trust, you really have nothing. Satan can do a lot with mistrust and jealousy. I knew in my heart I had to get away before this got nasty again.

It was during this time frame that Chris came through my drive through and informed me she was looking for office help. She offered me $1.50 more an hour than I was making at Dairy Queen. Without hesitation, I took her up on her offer.

One day on my way to pick the children up from my moms, I ran into Jimmy. The same Jimmy I'd kissed in the cooler when I was only 16.

Our eyes locked. I think he was just as shocked at seeing me as I was at seeing him. We both had our windows down. At the same time, we said each other's name in surprise.

He asked me to pull over up the road and he turned around when the traffic moved again. We stood and talked for about 15 minutes catching each other up on our lives.

He told me I looked great for our age. I was like, "Our age! I'm only 18, 19, 18, no 19, how old are we?" I questioned.

He laughed at me. He told me if I ever left Jeff he'd love to take me on a date. We went our separate ways that day but honestly Jimmy did not leave the back of my mind.

It was not long after that day when Jeff and I had another fight.

I went to my mom and explained to her how dangerous my situation was and that I needed a place to live. I was already paying her to baby-sit for me. I just needed a place to stay until I could get on my feet completely. I told her I was going to find a second job and I assured her I would quickly get out on my own.

She agreed to let me come live with her if that was what I felt was best. It was after William's first birthday when I moved in with my mother. She was in the process of planning her wedding to the guy who lived behind her. We were discussing me purchasing her home. I was excited for the first time in forever. I could afford to rent my mother's house on my own. With a roommate it would be even easier.

The thought that after a year or two I would also be in a position to purchase the home from her thrilled me to no end. Things were looking up for me.

I found a second job at night working as a waitress at a Steak n Shake in Nora. Jimmy had contacted me through Glidden Fence and we'd started dating even though I had not filed for a divorce yet.

I had been shopping for a lawyer and I was working on accumulating the $500 I had been told I'd need to file.

Jimmy made me feel beautiful and smart again. He made me laugh.

I justified sleeping with him before my divorce was legal because I had left Jeff and if I had the money I needed to file, I'd have filed for my divorce already. All of Jeff's worries regarding me being with someone else had finally become a reality.

One night when I came home from my second job, I walked in the front door and low and behold who was sitting on the couch but Jeff.

I froze in the doorway.

My mother was in her chair and she said, "Wendy, Jeff came here to talk to me about you and him. I know you are determined to file for a divorce but I think you should listen to him. After all you two have children together. Do you really want to short change your children of a life with both parents?"

Somehow I managed to move. I closed the door and sat down at the other end of the couch.

The gist was this: Jeff loved me. He felt awful about all that had gone wrong between us. He wanted another chance to make things right. If I still decided I wanted a divorce this time next year he'd pay for it. No questions asked. I was told to sleep on it.

My mom really pushed me to give him another try. After all, what did I have to lose? Was I going to be selfish like my father or would I put my family first?

I caved under the guilt.

Jimmy bowed out of the picture and wished me good luck with my marriage. He did not want to be the one to blame for its failure.

There were a couple major problems with this plan. One, being Jeff was an abusive person. Two, I had been with another man and he knew it.

A friend of mine was pregnant with her own first child. I knew she was around 5 months along when she arrived on my doorstep crying one night. She asked if we could go somewhere and talk. She saw the hesitation in my eyes and she told me briefly what she was crying over. I told Jeff I had to go with her. He was not happy to say the least but he allowed it. You see, my friend was currently dating a man of color and Jeff was as racist as a person could be back then. He did not want me associating with this girl, but with the news he was allowing an exception.

I took her down to the Pizza Hutt and we ordered some bread sticks. When I came back home Jeff attacked me from behind. He pushed me and called me a nigger lover.

I ran down the hall way to the bathroom and tried to close and lock the door. I didn't make it in enough time, he was right behind me.

Somehow I escaped the bathroom and ran to the other end of the house to our bedroom. I was a second too slow on getting the door closed again. He picked up a lamp that had no shade or shade holder and launched it at me.

I tried to jump out of the way but the lamp landed on my foot burning it and cutting it in the same instant. I screamed in pain. It was my howls that stopped Jeff from hurting me further.

Instantly he was crying and telling me it was all a mistake. I was numb. I had heard this too many times.

He called my mother and informed her we'd had a fight. He asked if she'd be willing to baby-sit the next night so we could have some alone time to work things out.

She agreed. I pretended to agree. I was done. I went to bed.

The next morning, I got up and continued pretending I was okay. I rode with him to work and when his crew pulled out I went home and packed up everything that was important to me and I took it to my grandmother's house. She was on Mackinac Island for the summer but she told me I was free to use her house.

Over the course of the next couple weeks Jeff was not allowed near me at work and he did not know where I was staying at night. I did not keep him from our children; he was able to visit them through my mother. He knew I wanted a divorce, but seeing how

I had not stuck to my end of the agreement, he was off the hook for having to pay for our divorce.

Again, I was shopping for a lawyer. Lena, my aunt by marriage, found me one for that only charged $250.00 for an uncontested divorce.

I met the man and paid him 1/2 down to get the ball rolling. I told him all I wanted was my maiden name back and custody of my children.

One night after work, there was a knock on the front door. When I went to answer it, I found Jeff standing there. He had followed me to my grandmothers from a safe distance.

My heart lurched. I slammed the door and locked it. I refused to let him in. He went home and called my grandma's house. Caller ID did not exist at the time so I answered the phone. It was Jeff. He informed me if I did not come home and talk to him he was going to set everything I'd left behind on fire.

I told him, "Enjoy the blaze." And I hung up. When I had left, I had taken everything that was important to me.

I finally got my own apartment in the fall of 1989 and my divorce decree was finalized on December 18, 1989.

I am happy to have made it this far in my retelling. I again am out of time to write and this is as good as any place to stop.

Today I pray for anyone who is in a dangerous situation. I pray you seek outside council. Get yourself some help. Things will never improve on their own. You need Christ.

Wendy, Mom of Many

Chapter 7

I'm learning to be the Light!

I used to shrink inside when people would say something about me being a Saint due to all the children I have had. I truly believed that if they knew the truth about my past, they would never call me by such a name.

I felt like such a fraud. In my mind, I was nowhere close to the description of a Saint.

I am my biggest critic. Over the years, I have given the evil one plenty of ammunition to fire against me. There is nothing like helping the destroyer of lives destroy you!

Now, when I find myself shrinking from something or having a moment of fear I swell with confidence. I say, "Oh, Satan, man you are good. You had me for a millisecond. Then I saw my fear for what it was. It is you filling me with fear because you are afraid of others seeing my light!"

If I'm where it's an option, I turn on some Christian music, or take out a devotional or even search the internet for inspirational bible quotes. Adding a coat of armor is never a bad thing!

I heard a tune today on my way to work that led me to know that today is the day I share one of my darkest moments. The song was talking about how we don't fall in an instant. How what used to be black and white slowly becomes gray. Instantly I was flashing on my past. I didn't change overnight. It was with each bad choice I made that I seemed to drift farther and farther away from who I was.

Over the course of time, as I went deeper and deeper down the road to hell, I convinced myself I could never return to the narrow path. I figured I had done way too much bad to ever be viewed as 'good enough' again. I truly believed I was an epic failure.

With that being said, let's get these dark ages of mine down on paper.

Prior to my divorce being approved by the judge, but well after it had been filed, Jimmy and I began seeing each other again. He was working at UPS and going to college, so his time for me was short and usually at crazy hours.

We had been seeing each other for about three months when I called over to his house. His father answered and was kind enough to inform me that Jimmy was on a date with his fiancée. My world reeled.

My roommate at the time worked at Apple Bees. I went there and sat in her station. When I arrived, I ran into one of her fellow buds. He was working the section next to hers. He caught me crying and he put everything he had into cheering me up.

Over the course of the next week he hung out with me when our schedules didn't clash. We ended up sleeping together. It was the first time I'd ever felt special. The event completely blew my mind! For the first time in my life, I finally realized what all the excitement was about when it came to being with someone intimately   .

My cycle was late and when I hadn't started by the following week, I took a pregnancy test. To my horror, it turned out to be positive.

This next truth is so awful. I know it is what held me back from telling this story. I had been with two men in one month. I had no idea which one was the father.

I was worried about how I would be judged for this. It was one thing to be called a slut and a whore when you knew you were not one. It was quite another thing to feel like you would be seen that way by everyone you knew. Can you imagine the gossip that would be created from my situation? It was more than I could bear. It kills me to admit as much, but it is the truth.

Once the baby was born there would be no question as to who the father was because Jimmy is white and Richard is black. I just could not endure the in-between.

Jimmy was engaged to another woman and honestly I had no desire to tell him I was pregnant but did not know if it was his or not. I did tell Richard about the dilemma I had found myself in though. After all, he was my friend.

He offered me an 'easy' solution. He would pay for my abortion. Even though I knew it was wrong to take a life, I convinced myself it was the best thing to do for all involved.

At the time the mantra was "This is your life" or "This is your body and your life". It was an acceptable thing to do.

I honestly want to puke reliving this because there was nothing okay about what I did. I knew life began at conception. I chose to ignore that truth and I took the easy way out. In the long run it was something that would haunt me for years and years.

My friend Donna, the same Donna I ran away with, drove me to the clinic and stayed with me.

The entire waiting room was full of women waiting their turn. I signed in and then I waited for my turn to see the counselor. I honestly don't know what the point of that was because there was no counseling.

I was called back to the room for the procedure and it was awful and painful. For me it was much worse than childbirth. It felt like I was being ripped apart.

Today, thanks to Planned Parenthood, we all know what happens to the baby inside of you during the abortion process. We know that the baby is capable of feeling pain and that it actually tries to get away from the vacuum that is sucking it out of its womb. I cannot begin to tell you how Satan used that information against me.

Richard came and stayed with me that first night. I don't know if I've ever been in more physical pain. At one point I hurt so badly I thought I might be dying. I know part of me wanted to die.

Richard and I had been friends up until then. I used to wonder what ever happened to us. Now I know. I pushed him away. Looking at him was too big of a reminder.

Jimmy called me after I had already gone through with my abortion. He was letting me know that he had enrolled himself in the Navy. I was so mad at him I told him I had been pregnant with his child and I had fallen and miscarried.

If he reads this book of mine, it will be the first time he has heard the truth about this pregnancy. I was angry at him and longed to hurt him. At the time, I blamed him for my emptiness. I reasoned that had he not deceived me, I would have never found myself in this situation. I blamed him for the predicament I had put myself in.

Please don't misunderstand what I am saying. This is not an excuse. I am just showing how far I had gone down the wide road. I wanted him to hurt as badly as I hurt. That is not our purpose

119

here on earth. However, it was where I was at in life by my own doing.

Very few people ever knew about this event. I even kept it out of my medical files.

Today I pray for those who have made the same choice I did. I pray that you are brought into the light and shown the truth. I also pray for those facing the decision of what to do when you find yourself pregnant and it was not your plan to become that way. I pray you are touched by a believer so deeply that you never have to face the demon of regret. I pray for all who want a baby yet cannot conceive. I thank God for Christ. I thank God for mercy and grace. In Jesus name I pray. Amen.

Wendy, Mom of Many

Chapter 8

The Only Baby I Ever Planned

After my abortion, I'd blown Jimmy off as well as avoided Richard at every turn until he stopped coming around at all.

I was working two jobs and raising two children on my own. The last thing in the world I was looking for was love and that's when I met Bruce Malone.

He had dark brown hair, gorgeous blue eyes and he stood over 6' tall. He was a walking talking dream of a guy. He was in college and he was on the basketball team.

He came over to my apartment one night and we ended up hitting it off. After less than 3 full months of dating, Bruce asked me to marry him.

I said, "Yes!"

From that point on, he non-stop begged me to have a baby with him.

I don't know why I thought it would take more than a couple tries for me to get pregnant but it didn't. I was pregnant the same month we began trying.

To save money so I could move to Iowa where Bruce was going to college, I moved in with my Aunt Janet and my Uncle Bob.

Bruce was supposed to be arranging us housing close to his campus. He only called me a couple times to update me on the progress and to see how the baby and I were getting along before

I received the next to last phone call I ever received from Bruce. Before I had a chance to even ask how he was doing, he said, "Wendy, I need to say this without interruption so just listen. I love you. I will always love you. This is too much. I'm not ready. My mom has moved and she changed her number, the college has moved me to a new dorm and they have been informed that you are not to have my new information. Don't bother my friends they know not to tell you anything. Good Luck." and he hung up on me.

I was frozen. I think I dropped the phone. Instantly my Aunt knew something was wrong. Through my tears, I shared what Bruce had said.

She thought it might be in the children's best interest to not see me in shambles. She suggested I go over to Lena and Jeff's house. They lived about 15 minutes away.

I really don't remember what all transpired over the next week or so other than the repo man showed up and towed off my car. I had not made a payment in 3 months.

With no car, no soon to be husband, no job and two children to somehow support on my own and another one on the way, my Aunt Janet had a heart to heart talk with me.

She asked me some really pointed questions. She wanted me to explain to her how I thought I would be able to provide for three children on my own when I was struggling to provide for only two children.

She asked me if I could honestly say I would never blame this child for how my life turned out.

She asked me if I thought it was fair to raise a baby on my own when I knew the father wanted nothing to do with his child.

In the end I decided that the fairest thing for all of the children concerned would be for me to give this baby to someone who was longing for a baby of their own. I was going to pick a couple to adopt my unborn child.

I contacted an adoption agency that allowed me to decide who the parents of my baby were going to be. I started with countless applications. I read resume after resume. In the end I narrowed it down to three couples. I requested to meet the couple I liked the best before making my final decision.

I wanted this baby to have a sibling. The couple I chose had a 4-year-old boy and they wanted him to have a sibling. I had read about that in their file.

I ended up deciding they were the ones I wanted to adopt my child. My baby's adoptive mother looked at me when the meeting was over and asked if I knew whether I was carrying a boy or a girl. I told her I did not know.

She confided that she would love a little girl but that she would be just as thrilled with another little boy. She was beaming as if she were carrying my child inside of her.

She next asked if I'd be okay with her touching my stomach and I said she could. My baby moved when she placed her hands on my belly and she got to feel it move. Her eyes filled with tears and she said, "Thank You".

Today I pray for all women and all babies that are longed for, miscarried, aborted, adopted and cherished alike. I pray for any and all the broken hearts damaged by the loss of a child. I give thanks that I know the children I gave back to God are with God as all unborn babies are. I pray peace over all with aching hearts. In Jesus name I pray. Amen. Wendy, Mom of Many

Chapter 9

Saying Goodbye to Amanda Rose Glidden

I ended the last chapter with the lady who was going to adopt my child telling me thank you. I remember attempting to smile at her. What happened next was something I was not expecting.

She leaned in a little closer almost as if it was a confidential promise and said, "What ever name you pick will be the name of your baby."

My world rocked. I had not allowed myself to pick out names for this baby. I don't remember how I got to the meeting and I don't remember how I got home. It's all blank.

I tried to keep my mind off the baby as much as a pregnant woman can. I kept busy. My mom had a paper route. Actually she had 3 routes. All 3 of them were walking routes. Every other day I delivered the papers on all 3 routes. It was part of my obligation. Honestly I didn't mind it at all. I truly enjoyed it. Fresh air. Exercise. It kept my mind off of my pregnancy. I just focused on apartment buildings and who in each building got the paper.

On Sundays we did the route together. It was good. During this time, my mom and I got along.

My original due date was March 6th. The irony of the date landing on my birthday was almost too much. I was relieved when they moved it to March 24th.

I arranged for Jeff to take care of Cassandra and William the weekend before my due date. I told him I would need him and his mom to keep them for approximately 3 weeks.

I woke up in labor on April 3, 1991, right in time for the paper route to be delivered. My mom checked my contractions and decided she had enough time to deliver her papers. I called Lena to let her know she needed to head our way.

By the time Mom got back from delivering papers it was time to head to the hospital. We got there and checked in. I was settled into a delivery room. A nurse came in and asked if I wanted an epidural. I said I did as I wanted to feel NOTHING. She assured me I'd be able to push but I wouldn't feel any pain.

I was asked if I wanted to hold the baby after it was born. I said no. I was too afraid to do that. I don't remember much about what we talked about while we waited. I remember someone coming in and checking on my progress and she popped my water. She stated, "That should speed things up."

My mom said, "Boy will it ever".

When she walked toward the door, my mom questioned, "Where are you going?"

She informed my mother that I was more than an hour away from delivering and she walked out of the room. Not even ten minutes later my mom ran out into the hallway to announce that the baby was coming and we needed assistance.

As often happens when I deliver, things are not in order and it gets pretty crazy. In no time flat I gave birth. The doctor held up my baby and announced, "We have a girl." She weighed in at 9lbs 6oz

I was taken clear on the other side of the hospital because I had requested not to be in the maternity ward. Lena came with me. When my nurse came to check on me, I asked if it was okay if I walked around.

She said, "If you feel up to it but be careful."

I said I would. When she left, I looked at Lena and said, "I can't stand it. You want to go see her?"

She said, "Yes!"

We walked out of my room, smiled at the girls at the desk, and went around the corner right into the elevator. We went down and then across to the maternity ward through a tunnel.

The nurse in the nursery was just getting ready to feed her and she asked if I would like to give my baby her bottle. I could not stop myself. I had to hold her. I fed her, I admired her, and I sang to her. I inhaled her newborn sent.

Every fiber of my being wanted to keep her in my arms. Right then I looked up and my personal nurse was looking at me through the glass. She motioned for me to come out. She greeted me with a wheel chair and said, "Child when I said you could walk around, I did not mean for you to take a mile hike. You could bleed to death you know. We need to check your vitals."

I gave my baby back to the nursery nurse and sat in the wheelchair.

I went back again and again to hold her and feed her. I thought long and hard about what to name her. I always loved the name Amanda and I hadn't picked that name before because Jeff's sister already had an Amanda.

For her middle name I decided on Rose. It was my Grandmother's first name and I thought that she was as beautiful as a rose.

I filled out her birth certificate and filled out the final paperwork numbly. I was informed they had received Bruce's sign off. I knew that they had found him for he called me to inquire as to whether the papers he'd been served were legit or not. He wanted to make sure that I was not trapping him into paying child support.

I told him I was giving the baby up for adoption and that the papers were not a trick. I was shocked they had found him. However, I was not the least bit surprised when they told me he had signed off on the adoption.

I was released 24 hours before Amanda was due to be released. When I came back to the hospital to hold her one more time, thinking I would be able to give her one last bottle, I was informed I had just missed her by fifteen minutes.

I have no idea how I walked back to the car. Inside I felt like dying. When I finally made it home, I fell apart.

Today I pray for all birth moms whose hearts ache. May our baby's know we love them. May they never doubt that. May we feel at peace with our decisions. In Jesus name I pray. Amen.

Wendy, Mom of Many

Chapter 10

The Aftermath

When I woke up the next morning, I was instantly in tears again. I got up and walked into Cassy and Billy's bedroom. I stood there for a moment and then I began tearing their room down. I took apart their bunk bed. I pulled out the rest of their furniture and toys. Next I took out the carpet. Then I began painting the walls.

By the time my mom got home from work, I had put the room completely back together. I did all of those things three days after giving birth. I could not stand to sit still because as soon as I did my mind went straight to Amanda and then I would begin crying all over again.

I must have thought about contacting the adoption agency and telling them I had changed my mind a million times.

I decided it was time for me to find a job. I had no car so I walked. First I went to Kroger and put in an application. I also stopped off at the Liquor store on the corner and filled out an application. After that I walked and walked and walked. I ended up at Glendale Mall and went to the bookstore. I gazed at the covers of a lot of books but I don't think my eyes actually read any of them. I was trying everything in my power to NOT think about Amanda and I was failing. I walked back home before the sun set.

The next day I decided to walk in another direction and I ended up seeing a sign at a Dairy Queen asking for help. I went in, filled out an application and was lucky enough to score a job interview.

The owner hired me saying his decision was based mostly on my smile. I thought that was so ironic because my smile was completely fake. It never reached my eyes or my heart. Regardless, I was hired. I told him I could start immediately so I was scheduled to come in the next evening. I was happy to have something to help keep me busy so I didn't have to think.

Within two weeks of starting at Dairy Queen, I had an interview at Kroger. I was originally hired as Deli help during the day.

I purchased a bicycle for me to travel back and forth to work. My mother worked during the day so I had located a daycare I could afford. My mother agreed to watch the children in the evening when I worked. Everything was going according to plan. I was keeping myself so busy I did not have a lot of time to dwell on the emptiness that was enveloping me. Within a couple more weeks I ended up moving from Night manager to Store Manager at Dairy Queen. Ironically at the same time I was moved from Deli to 2nd Baker at Kroger and the hours worked out perfectly.

I was working from 10 AM to 10 PM at Dairy Queen. I would bike home, take a shower and get into my Kroger uniform and bike there. I worked at Kroger from 11 at night until 7 in the morning. The next day I began my routine all over again. Feed the children breakfast and then take them to their daycare. I then returned the car to my mom, and rode my bike to work. I worked 6 days a week at Dairy Queen. I baked 2 nights in a row at Kroger and then I would get three nights off. I was working myself to exhaustion and that was the way I liked it.

Within a month of holding the 2nd Baker position, the Head Baker quit at Kroger and I was moved up to her position. Now I was working three nights on, two nights off and 3 nights on again at Kroger and still 6 days on one day off at Dairy Queen.

I began taking a drug for energy. I had found them in a magazine. The pills were called Black Beauties. They helped me stay awake on that 3rd night. I liked being so overworked for the mere fact that when I finally got the chance to sleep, it did not take me long to get there.

I kept up this routine for almost 3 months! That was when my 2nd baker quit and instead of sleeping after working 72 hours straight, I had to go in to bake a 4th night. I don't know what I was thinking that night, but I ended up taking six black beauties during my shift. By the time the night was over, all I could think about was how badly I wanted to go to sleep. It was my day off from Dairy Queen. I had every intention of going home and crashing.

I clocked out, jumped on my bike and headed home. I was speeding so hard on the black beauties that I was flying on my bike. I never saw that pot hole, but it stopped me in my tracks. I flew over the handle bars and landed face first in Keystone Avenue.

When the lights came back on courtesy of smelling salts, I found myself staring up at a fireman who was leaning down into my face. He asked me, "Do you hurt anywhere?"

I managed to say, "My face." and tears began flowing from my eyes.

He said, "It's bad, but I have seen worse."

My whole body hurt. In the distance I heard a woman hysterically telling someone, I had broken my neck.

I tried to turn to look at her but I could not move. For a moment I panicked thinking I might be paralyzed then I realized I was strapped down on a stretcher. The fireman got my attention again and said, "I am going to start touching you beginning at your shoulders. Let me know what hurts."

As soon as he touched my arm I winced. Without hesitation he cut the sleeve on my shirt. I also winced when he got to my hip and again, an article of my clothing was cut.

I lived 3 doors down from the firehouse. They knew who I was. They had already notified my mother and she arrived shortly after I had come to. The firemen loaded me up in the ambulance against my wishes. I insisted I was fine. Just a little banged up. I pleaded with them to let me go home. I told them all I wanted was to go home, but my mother felt I needed to be checked out. The firemen thought I might have broken some bones.

I ended up having ex-rays for almost every part of my body on the right side. As it turns out, I had only taken a chip out of my skull right above my eye socket. I had also given myself a major concussion. Other then those two things, I just had severe bruising.

My eye ended up swelling shut and it remained that way for over 10 days before I could get it to open a sliver. My face was so black and blue it remained bruised for over a month.

It is funny how many women will tell you, "You need to leave that man!" when you look like I did. At first, I tried to tell them there was no man. I explained that I had done this to myself in a bike wreck.

They would look at me with pity and say, "Honey, we've heard it all before. You need to leave him."

After about a week of this, I began informing them that I had already left him.

My mom was so mad at me for almost literally working myself to death. Before I even knew it she had taken my pills out of my room. She told me, "You gave up Amanda so that you could be the best mom you could be to Cassy and Billy and all you have done is work yourself almost literally to death."

She was right. She insisted I pick one job and deal with my choice because she believed my reasons had been well thought out.

Today I pray for all who have heartache for whatever reason. I pray you turn to God and ask Him to help heal your heart. I pray you are strong enough to lean on others. I also pray for those who minister to the heartaches of others. I pray we always allow the Holy Spirit to work through us. In Jesus name I pray. Amen.

Wendy, Mom of Many

Chapter 11

Back Flash: Why I Believe Bruce Left Me

I know heartache. I am familiar with the thoughts that it would be easier to go to sleep and never wake up again. That is what the evil one wants you to believe. It is a lie.

Life always has twists and turns. Aren't you the least bit interested in what may be around the next corner? Tomorrow might just be the best day of your life!

In Chapter 8; The Only Baby I Ever Planned, I shared how Bruce had called me saying that this was all too much for him and he had changed his mind. In the heat of writing that, I was still in the same mental shape I was in the first time I lived those moments.

I was confused and full of overwhelming heart ache. I just could not wrap my brain around it all. I had never thought to put myself in Bruce's shoes.

Recently I have had many back flashes and they have not been pleasant to say the least. Somehow I knew I'd have to talk about the torment I lived through after I divorced Jeff. I now understand what it was that was too much for Bruce and in my heart I can no longer be angry at him. Allow me to paint the scene.

My divorce from Jeff was far from easy or pleasant and the repercussions of leaving him continued off and on until our children were teenagers. Anyone that has ended a relationship knows full well the battle that often ensues do to each parties hurts. This relationship was one of those. I think it happens more in abusive situations than others.

If you have never been in a physically abusive relationship and you know someone who is currently in one, you may question why this person stays there. Perhaps you wonder why they don't leave. You may wonder why they go back. I don't. I know why. You see, I was that girl.

It was towards the end of the summer. Cassy and William still had a couple weeks left to spend with their father during summer vacation. I was enjoying the morning with Bruce when my phone rang. Brenda, Jeff's mom was on the other end.

"Wendy, Jeff moved a couple weeks ago. He hasn't let any of us know where he moved to. I think he is in Jasper. I think him and Jodi are planning on keeping the children. He hasn't even let me have any contact with them for two weeks and I'm worried they may move further. I should have called you the day they moved off my property but I thought he would let me know their new address. I am so sorry."

My heart dropped as I told her she was okay. I hung up the phone and told Bruce I needed to locate my children before Jeff knew I had been alerted to the situation.

He decided to come along. I grabbed pictures of both Cassandra and William and verified that I had a copy of our legal certified divorce decree in the car.

Three hours later we arrived in the middle of Jasper. I went into a local gas station, armed with the pictures of my children and asked if anyone had seen either of them. The attendant who was working said she did not recognize either of them, but by the grace of God a lady inside the store did. She told me they lived in an apartment complex down the street from her. I came out of the gas station feeling hopeful and headed in the direction she had pointed me in. Sure enough there were two sets of apartments back to back just like she had said. She had no idea which unit they were in but she said she had seen the children playing

134

outside just the other day.

I went to the first door and knocked on it. A girl answered the door. I showed her the pictures of Cassy and Billy and asked if she knew which unit my children were in. Again, by the Grace of God she did.

I walked around the building to the other side and knocked on the door she had indicated.

Jodi, Jeff's new wife, opened the door and promptly attempted to slam it shut. I put my foot in the opening and it was smashed between the door and the frame. I bit my lip and closed my eyes for a second.

As she attempted to kick my foot out of the way to close the door, she shouted "We are getting custody of your children and you will never see them again."

I pushed the pain out of my mind and shoved the door open. Once inside, I called out, "Cassy, Billy where are you?"

They came racing down the stairs. I immediately noticed a gigantic scab on William's face. As calmly as I could, I asked, "Where are your clothes?"

They excitedly said, "Up here!" and they ran back up the stairs.

I walked by Jodi and went up the stairs. The majority of their belongings were still in the laundry basket I had sent them in. I picked up the basket but did not immediately see their shoes anywhere.

I asked William how he had gotten the boo on his face.

Cassy answered, "Jodi did it. She grabbed him by his arm and yanked him into this door."

I was astounded by the severity of the wound. I picked up the basket deciding I would need to buy new shoes and I told the children, "Let's go".

Jodi was in the hallway attempting to block my path. She told me, "You can not take the children with you."

I chuckled and very calmly walked toward her saying, "That's where you would be wrong."

As I walked forward, she walked backward.

"You will never lay a hand on either one of them again." I said as I continued toward the steps.

She could have stepped aside, but she did not. Why she continued walking backwards is your guess as much as mine. I will admit I took great pleasure in watching as she lost her balance and tumbled down the stairs. I never had to lay one finger on her.

I helped the children around her and we went out the door. Bruce was standing in the entry way. He never said a word the entire time I was inside. I placed William and Cassandra in the car, put their belongings in the back and told Bruce to drive as I climbed into the passenger side.

Jodi managed to get to the door and I watched as she ran to the neighbors screaming, "Call the police."

I think perhaps she must have reconsidered that option due to her abusing William so badly for the police never came after us nor did they ever contact me.

It was shortly after that day that I moved in with my Aunt and Uncle while Bruce went to Iowa to locate us a place. As you know, Bruce never found a place for us. Instead, he ended our relationship.

Today, I understand how crazy that whole scene must have been for him. I now think that what he could not handle was the severity of the drama.

Side note: Cassy was recently living in Huntingburg, Indiana. To visit her, I had to drive through Jasper. In retrospect, I am amazed at how quickly I found them that day. I am blessed that I found them so quickly. I am also blessed that Jeff was not there when I showed up. I KNOW God helped me that day. Even though I had felt unworthy of being loved by God at that time of my life, I clearly see how Faithful He was and truly always is. What a loving Father we are blessed to have. I am overwhelmed with gratitude. Thank you Father for your faithfulness. Every time I have knocked you have answered. My only regret is how long it took me to fully come back home. I thank you for never shutting me out.

Today I come before you Father asking for more strength and clarity on how I am to share all of this. I thank you for getting me through every rough spot I have been in. I thank you for your Grace. Where would I be without it? I stand in awe of how you have led me to writing again. I thank you for all my education over the years. I thank you for helping me find fellowship. I pray Father that anyone secluded from others find fellowship with fellow believers. I also pray for all who are living in an abusive situation. Please lift them up. Fill them with the Faith you filled me with the last time Father. Thank you for being forever faithful. Thank You for answering every time I banged on the door. Thank You for loving me even when I did not love myself. I am blessed beyond measure. So many women are going through something like this right now. So many abusers so many abused. I know you love them all Father. I ask that you speak to all your children Father. Fill the dark corners of the world with light. Send hands and feet to those who do not yet know the good news. Whisper your love to the hearts of all your children Father, found and lost alike. In Jesus name I pray, Amen. Wendy, Mom of Many

137

Chapter 12

Revenge is NOT Sweet!

If you recall the chapter How I came to know God from the first book in this series, you know that I had been caught smoking cigarettes as a child. While being punished for it and at the threat of being further punished by my father, I had prayed to God. When I came before my father he had elected to not punish me due to a feeling that he didn't need to. I knew it was God that had saved me from harm and I had promised to never smoke cigarettes again as long as I lived.

So here I was, age 22, still alive but honestly dead inside. After my bike wreck my mother had forced me to pick one job and I had chosen Dairy Queen.

I ended up dating a guy from work and within a couple of months he moved in with me. I threw a New Year's Eve party at my home for all my employees and a couple of my friends.

I did not know that the guy living with me had made out with another one of my employees that night after he had left me for her. Then, as often happens, everyone steps forward to share what they knew about the situation.

You could say what I learned made me angry as if I needed any help in that direction. I was so tired of being hurt by men I honestly was out to hurt a man myself.

That spring I did some really crazy stuff. Any guy that asked me out, I agreed to allow him to take me on a date. I was not myself on my dates. I gave nothing and took what they had to offer. I

was even a little mean about it all. I went out to eat, out to movies and then I would simply dismiss them at my door and never answer their call again. I was just out to use them. After all, I figured in the end that was what they had intended to do to me.

All the while my irritation grew at my ex and my ex-friend. Yes, the girl that had taken my man was supposedly a friend. I don't know why I ended up doing what I ended up doing and in no way am I proud of it, but let's just dive into the heart of what went down.

I was on my way down to French Lick to pick my children up from their visit to their dad's when I stopped in at a gas station. I very badly wanted to be out of my head for a moment. I did not do drugs or drink at the time, but I recalled cigarettes would give you a funny feeling. In the heat of the moment I bought a pack and a lighter. I got outside opened them up, got one out and lit it. I remember looking up at the heavens and calling out to God in my thoughts, "I'm breaking my promise. What are you going to do about it?"

Of course no lightening bolt came down from heaven. I was convinced God couldn't care less. A big part of me seriously wished a lightning bolt would have struck me and put me out of my misery but one did not.

I never intended on becoming a smoker when I lit that first one for I hated everything about cigarettes, but I remained a smoker for two decades! At first I only had a couple puffs at night but within that first year that changed to smoking at work, in the car and wherever I was.

Shortly after I began smoking cigarettes, I ran into the so called friend that had stolen my guy and to this day I don't know why I did what I did, but I know I did it. I pretended that I was happy she and my ex were happy together and planning on getting married.

She invited me over for a hang out and I went. You could say he was surprised to see me. I played very non-nonchalant that first visit. Next, I was invited to a party they were throwing and I went hell bent on breaking them up

Before the night was over I had slept with her man who was originally my man and then on my way out the door, I proudly informed her of what had happened and I left. The next morning, I woke up feeling horrible about the situation. I remember walking into the bathroom and clearly hearing; "Is revenge sweet?"

"No," I answered to an empty room, "It is very bitter."

This was not one of my proudest moments. I did not understand then why I had done something so against my character. Just because she had done it to me first did not make my actions okay.

Today, I know that I allowed my emotions; anger, resentment, bitterness just to name a few, to take over. That is all the evil one needs to use us against each other and use me he did. From here I just sank further and further into the pit of hell.

My feelings about myself were reeled into even more darkness for this same man showed up at my house crying saying he loved me and wanted me back. He knew I was inside because my car was in the drive way. I knew he did not truly love me, but I was freaked out by it all. I did not take him back. I didn't even open my front door.

I almost ended up going back to Jeff after this incident. I was so sure all men were rotten and I was beginning to believe I was under some curse for trying to out wit God and then not staying in my marriage. I thought I was supposed to go back to Jeff and live with him until death do us part. I ended up seeing him a few times and very quickly realized I'd rather be dead then spend the rest of my life un-cherished and unloved than be with someone I did not truly love myself.

My advice to anyone dealing with rejection, heartache, jealousy, anger, resentment, or any other emotion not tied to Love, is this; Give it to God and let it go. Don't allow it to eat you alive, literally. The evil one loves these emotions. He will use you as a weapon. Don't allow that to happen. Trust me when I say; Revenge is not sweet at all. Twenty years later, I would love the opportunity to tell that girl I am sorry.

Father, today I pray for all hurting hearts. I pray that they come to you and give up those emotions that bring no goodness with them. I thank you Father for taking me back. My outright defiance and rudeness to you would be acts undeserving of forgiveness but that is not the type of Father you are. I am so blessed to be so loved by you. I know you are always with me and I know you are always faithful and I am so very thankful for that Father. As I see how far I have come, I get choked up. For in seeing, I also see clearly the love you hold for your children. May more of my brothers and sisters also begin to see that truth about you Father. In Jesus name I pray. Amen.

Wendy, Mom of Many

You Are Worthy Too

Angels, Answers,

Signs and Wonders

By Wendy Glidden

Copyright 2014 Wendy Glidden

Dear Reader,

Today is March 18, 2014. That would make it Totally
Terrific Testimonial Tell All Tuesday! This is my tell all: It
was my belief that the third book God put on my heart to
publish would be out before the end of this month. So
many obstacles have occurred since the editing process for
You Are Worthy Too: Marriage, Motherhood & My Moral
Meltdown began that I am not sure You Are Worthy Too:
Angels, Answers, Signs & Wonders will be available before
months' end. I do know the evil one does not want this one
to hit the shelves.

An element I had wondered how I would write is what I
have written this morning. In each book, I include a Dear
Reader letter. I feel it lets you, the reader, know I truly have
heart in the game. It is a more personal call out than the
true life events I share.

With this book I was not sure what I was meant to say in
my dear reader letter. I knew of one thing that needed to be
a part of my letter, but how to take that and stretch it into a
letter when it was simply a single truth, well that was an
entirely different matter. That brings me to today:

This morning I knew God wanted me up early. When Mike
woke me up at 5:15 AM to ask if I had seen his gloves, I
went to look for them. I asked him where he had last seen
them and he insisted he had left them in his helmet and
now they were gone!

I wasn't angry at all that he'd woken me up because I
already knew in my heart that God wanted me up. In my

sleepiness and honestly disobedience I was trying to deny what I felt to be the case.

When Mike decided we had looked everywhere that the children may have hidden his gloves, he apologized for getting me up so early. I confessed that God wanted me up anyway so he had done me a favor as I was being disobedient. I went on to say to Mike that I was pretty sure he had been used to force me to get up. He kind of laughed me off until he went to leave. When he went to put his helmet on his head, he discovered his gloves inside.

He looked at me astonished and said, "God really did want you up."

Everything about this morning makes me smile. It is God that took away the pain that made me dread each morning. That in itself is a wonder. I still hurt a little ~ perhaps a gentle reminder of how life used to be.

I marvel at God and His ways. We all often complain about how God works as well as His timing. We do not see how weak willed we truly are in our own flesh.

In all honesty, God has been extremely patient with me. All awful moments in my life were never the end of the world. They were just awful moments. I also have many moments I treasure. They are the ones I feel God put on my heart to share within this collection of true life events.

My next book coming out will be entitled 'In the Midst of Spiritual Warfare'. Originally, I thought it would be my second book. I was on my way to church one day when I saw the cover and heard the title. However, it has slid back to being my fourth book. After this last month, I think that the reason it went from number two to number four was because God was prepping me to write about a topic that I was about to experience hard core. I truly feel that I am more prepared to write what God wants in it than I was prior to the battles I have faced in the last 40 days!

I have been under the craziest attacks since I began piecing this book together. In every way I have been under assault.

It has been eye opening amazing to watch God come through for me in all aspects. Each time, no matter what has come my way, I have found myself no worse off and perhaps even a step ahead, as I have continually walked faithfully in the Spirit, come what may.

I find myself instantly praying as I have felt myself pulled away from the fruit of the Spirit. I quickly call upon God to carry me through. Calling upon Him keeps me from fret and worry. As I am bombarded with fiery arrows, I lift my shield of faith and distinguish them. By being on alert and picking up my sword, I have protected myself as God has instructed me to do. By recognizing the enemy at work and being dressed for battle, I go into the fight calling out, "My Lord help me."

I pray as you read this book what you walk away with is an unshakeable faith. A faith that anytime anything in your life begins to take place that causes your heart to panic or

you begin to fret, or when any form of fear or distress weigh in upon you, you find yourself on your knees. You do not always have to be on your knees in a physical sense but that is your posture in a heartfelt sense.

You will recognize that force of fear upon you pressing deeply and you will pray in a way that you speak from your heart and He will answer.

If you have read my first two books you know I was no 'angel'. Yet, when I was at the end, knowing on my own I was not going to make it, I called upon the Lord from my knees and He answered me. Me. He answered me!

I was desperate, and I was seeking. I wanted help but did not fully believe that I was worthy of helping. I did not realize quite yet that I was forgiven. It took me a couple of years to believe I was a redeemed Child of God. It took me reading His word, joining two bible studies, going to church, listening to teachers on Moody Radio, singing songs of praise courtesy of K-Love and being sponsored to attend the Great Banquet to have that light come on.

We all have a way out of this place that many truthfully call hell. I get why so many refuse to believe that God is in Heaven cheering them on. I too believed I had fallen too far to ever be picked back up let alone thought of. That is a lie!

If you seek, you will find, but you truly have to seek. You have to give God the best of you every day. You have to rely on Him when trouble hits. As you do these things you allow Him to show Himself to you.

We are blind to the heavenly realm. It is beyond our understanding. It just is. I have been blessed to have seen both a person and my Winnebago shrouded in indescribable lights, as if surrounded in a ceiling of diamonds and crystals. I wish that mental image did due justice to the lights of Heaven but it truthfully doesn't. It is much more captivating than you can imagine.

I leave you with a smile on my face this morning for I have fretted about what I was going to put in my dear reader letter. It is, after all, a very important component of all my books. I want you to know I am truly interested in helping you find your unwavering faith. It is a vital part of your armor and in my opinion one of the coolest elements of your suit!

As you read my book you will see that I have had run ins with angels. As a word of caution, do not get caught up in the angels themselves. Remember that it is God that created them. Should you find yourself amazed or curious about them, be more amazed and curious about their Maker. He is the one that sends the angels to you.

I pray this book finds you building your own relationship with the Lord. In the beginning it says He walked in the Garden of Eden with Adam and Eve in the cool of the day. As a child, I too walked with God. I talked His ear off and asked many questions. It was when I mistrusted Him that I cut myself off from Him.

I truly was that teenager with the worst attitude toward my loving Father for over a decade. Then for two more decades I was convinced I had to find a way to work my way to forgiveness and worthiness. I was so lost. The truth was hidden from me by my own misunderstanding and lack of effort.

Please don't repeat my behavior then. Repeat my behavior now. For as boldly as I talked to God as a child, I talk to Him today. As much as I depended on Him then, I depend on Him now. He is my Lord and Savior and He loves me. Should I be weak, I call upon Him for strength. When I feel myself becoming who I once was through anger or frustration, I quickly realize I am walking in the flesh, and I do not like how it feels at all. I give my situation to God and let it go. Often I walk away for a moment and quickly call out to God to help me with my tongue. I pray you get here too, because here is where life becomes amazing.

With that, I leave you with this final statement; Be blessed AND BE A BLESSING

Love, Wendy Glidden

Chapter 1

Transported

I know there are times in my life when I wish I could be picked up and transported some where else. I am sure many of us have had at least one moment in our lives when this has been the case.

Once, I really was transported. I did not really know what happened at the time and the friend I was with was so freaked out by the incident, that she was gripping the steering wheel and told me she did not want to discuss what had gone down.

Allow me to paint the scene:

It was a Friday night in the summer of 1993. Tami and I were headed down to French Lick for the weekend. I was getting ready to move down there in a couple of weeks. I had put in my notice at Glidden Fence. Chris and I had agreed that it was not healthy for us to work together any longer.

At the moment I was pregnant for the fifth time in my life and I was planning on aborting the pregnancy the following week. It is not pretty but it is the truth.

I was going to go to Ohio to have the abortion done this time because they offered to gas you and it was a much nicer facility. The first time I had elected to terminate a pregnancy, I had gone to a clinic in Indianapolis.

I knew there was no way I could go through with it if I had to do it that way again. However, knowing I could go somewhere that offered to gas its patients so that they would not be fully aware of what was going on made the option doable in my mind.

I justified that if I had this baby, the father would never leave me be. After having to deal with Jeff over our children, and knowing how this guy was with his own children and their mothers, I just was not interested in having him attempt to control my life via a child.

I am not sure if my decision and what it opened me up to was why what happened that night happened. I have wondered if I was about to face something tragic that night more than once. I imagine I will not know all of the details of that crazy night until I am on the other side. For now, this is all I know:

The sun was on its way down and we wanted to make up for lost time. Tami and I had been shown a shortcut a couple of times and we were sure with the two of us we could maneuver the back roads on our own. We turned off of SR 37 and headed west.

We had driven in the same direction for about 10 minutes when out of nowhere the craziest animal I have ever seen appeared in the road. He was as long as the car and his face seemed to be at eye level with where we sat.

For twenty years, I was sure Tami had jerked the wheel and somehow kept us on the road around a turn off I had never seen. I thought this was the case because as we were truly spun, I found myself face to face with this thing through the passenger side window. I was stunned that this creature seemed to smile at me. He was so demonic looking. I'm not sure if my brain has ever identified anything else as demonic in the instant my eyes landed on it. If I was to categorize it, I would place it in the canine category but it was not like any dog I have ever seen.

I turned to Tami and said, "Did you see that demon dog smile at us?"

Tami's face was as white as a ghost and her fingers clasped the steering wheel so tightly they too were white. "I don't want to talk about it." Tami said adamantly.

I sat back in my seat wondering what on earth that animal had been. With Tami not wanting to talk about the demonic looking dog like creature, I did not think I should pester her with questions regarding her thoughts and her driving skills while she was driving. I truly wanted to ask her how she had managed to turn the car so quickly. I hadn't even seen a side street to turn onto when the demon dog leapt in front of us.

We drove on in silence for approximately another 15 minutes without any sign of a town. I think both of us were beginning to think we may be lost. There was no turning around. Neither one of us wanted to run into that demonic creature again.

Within a few minutes after deciding we were going to continue driving in the direction we were going, we saw signage indicating we were coming up to a stop sign. As we got closer I think we both gasped. We found ourselves directly across from the Coca Cola Plant on SR 37.

The distance between the Coca Cola Plant and where we had turned off the road would take a person a little over thirty minutes to drive straight down SR 37 at over 55 miles per hour.

We had not been traveling that quickly as we were unfamiliar with the road we were traveling down and it was dark now.

While I thought we had been traveling south and Tami thought we had continued traveling west, we had ended up driving for approximately 25 minutes on a back road well west of SR 37 and had found ourselves not only back north at least 30 miles on SR 37, we were on the east side of the road. There is no way to go over or under that road anywhere along that stretch of highway. The whole thing was unexplainable. We had turned off of SR 37

151

and we had headed west away from it. We never crossed it again until we came up on it from the east.

No matter which way you looked at it, with the time we had for travel, there was no way we could have traveled to where we had found ourselves without some serious help.

There was no other explanation outside of the fact that we had somehow been transported away from that demon dog. But why? What did it all mean? I was intrigued and Tami was spooked.

I think we sat in silence staring at that Coca Cola plant for an entire minute before I said, "How on earth?"

"I don't know. I don't want to talk about it. It's impossible." Tami answered.

"We never crossed 37 Tami, how did we end up so far on the other side and all the way back here? It doesn't make sense." I reiterated.

"I know. I don't know. I don't want to think about it." Tami said and put the car back in motion. "We aren't taking that short cut ever again."

"Fine by me." I stated. That was the craziest looking dog I had ever seen and I had no desire to cross its path again.

Over the last couple of decades, I have shared this story with only a couple of people. I had so many questions and really wanted to tell Tami how impressed I was with how she had kept the car on the road but had not pushed the topic. Truthfully, the opportunity had never come up. That was until last year. Tami and I were hanging out more often. One night, Tami, Ladonna, a mutual friend of ours, and I were all hanging out.

I had driven straight there from bible study and it just so

happened on that night, while studying Acts, my group came across the section where Phillip was snatched away by the Spirit of the Lord and was teleported away after sharing the truth of Jesus Christ being the Son of God and baptizing a Eunuch.

Jordan made mention that there are a couple of reports in the bible where someone was picked up and transported away.

I sat straight up and shared what had happened to me that fateful night years ago

When I left bible study, I headed to Tami's and happened to catch her and Ladonna finishing up an episode of Buffy, the vampire slayer. I could not resist the moment. I looked at Tami and said, "Explain to me how you can watch this scary stuff without a problem and even read Stephen King thrillers but refuse to discuss the craziest thing that I believe either one of us has ever been a part of in real life?"

Ladonna spoke up and asked Tami, "What is she talking about?"

Tami looked at Ladonna and said, "When you hang out with Wendy, crazy stuff can happen."

She then began telling Ladonna the story and when she got to the dog, I chimed in and said, "And Tami jerked the wheel so hard, my face was pressed to the passenger window and I was looking right at this demon dog and I'm positive it smiled at us"

Tami said, "Wen, I never turned the wheel."

I was like, "What? I swear you jerked that car so hard you pressed me up against the door. I was face to face with that thing"

Tami insisted, "Wendy, I never turned the car."

I was truly surprised by her side of the story, but decided that we were moved so swiftly and truly were turned around and placed on another road going in a complete opposite direction that I must have felt the shift. I don't know why I was allowed to feel that and Tami was not.

We finished sharing the rest of the story and left it at that. I told Tami, I had learned that people had truly been transported in the bible and that must have been what happened to us.

I still have no idea what that demon dog was up to, I am just thankful that God removed us from the situation.

I will admit when I first began putting this book together, I kept getting drawn to this event and fought having it become a part of this book because I did not understand the lesson I was meant to learn or the reason for the event. That is when I remembered that we are told we are not able to understand everything that happens to us in this world.

We are not meant to focus so much on the why's but more on the creator and in trusting that He is faithful and is always keeping us from absolute destruction.

There are so many things that could have gone wrong that night. People wreck their cars into trees and die for all kinds of crazy reasons. We had a great reason to wreck a car and yet that is not what happened. Tami and I were kept from whatever harm was waiting for us.

Today, I pray that whatever you are going through, you pause long enough to just talk to God. He is your father. He longs for a relationship with you. From the moment Adam and Eve were separated from God, He extended them grace and began forming a way to reconcile Himself back with His children.

You are a child of God. The only thing keeping you separated from having a relationship with Him would be you. You alone must knock for Him to answer. I believe that option has to do with Free Will. Another gift He gave us.

I encourage you to reflect upon your life; the good as well as the good in the midst of the bad. It is my belief, should you look with clear eyes, you will catch a glimpse of God at your side through it all. Blessings to all who try.

Wendy, walks with God, Mom of Many

Chapter 2

Knowledge Bestowed Upon Me in College!

Recently I found myself praying for knowledge. I knew it was available. I'm just not the best at finding it on my own. I've been pretty good at the whole self education thing my entire life. Knowledge and self education are two different things though.

When I attended St Pius X Catholic School in my seventh and eighth grade years, my math teacher put me into independent study. Within those two years, working at my own pace, I completed Algebra I, Geometry and was on my way through Algebra II. No one pushed me except me. I have always loved math and English.

Advanced Chemistry was one of the hardest classes I attended in high school. I took it my junior year. I just could not grasp what the teacher was trying to get us to understand. It did not help that she was using another book to teach out of. Your notes were supposed to carry you through, but for the life of me I could not grasp what was on the board! I was struggling to say the least. I knew if I did not get my grade up, I was going to be in trouble.

It had happened to me my freshman year of high school in advanced biology class. Mr. Denari refused to round up. Had he not been so strict in his stance, my grade would have been a B- that first quarter. Instead it was a C+.

I was so distraught over the grade on my first quarter report card that I made him write my grade point average and a note regarding the fact that he would not round up in his class on my report card. I'm not sure many teachers have had the privilege of seeing a student cry over tenths of a point.

I insisted he write on my report card that if I was in any other class, the teacher would have rounded up and given me a B-.

He did agree to do that much for me. However, the end result at home was the same. A grade listed as a C+ was not a B- no matter what. I tried to point out the truth about the grade point average and the side note from Mr. Denari. It made no difference.

Now, back to the chemistry class, I didn't really consciously pray for help with my advanced chemistry class. It was more of a desperate thought plea from my heart. God knows everything about you to your very core. A simple thought can be counted as a prayer.

I was thinking pretty hard about that class and that grade and completely lost as to how I could get it up for I had not one lick of understanding in that class room. Then, the next day in class, my teacher wrote something on the board and everything clicked. I knew in my heart I had done some of this work before only it had all seemed much simpler.

I was a pack rat back in those days. Everything I had ever written, I had kept. I went home and rummaged through my science notes from the seventh and eighth grade and low and behold there it all was.

I never struggled in that class again. I did not use my high school chemistry book. Instead I used my seventh and eighth grade science notes and brought my grade from a D to a solid B! Self education at its best!

I have yet to write anything much about age 24 - 34. There is a book there if not two. This would be a chapter from that era.

I was 25 years old and living in Florida. Up to this point I had never had a hard time landing a job. However, in 1994 while residing in Florida I could not get hired to save my life. I couldn't even land a cashier job and I had experience!

There was one thing holding me back. I had not one lick of experience using computers. My fear of them was so ridiculous I wouldn't even step foot in a library in Florida because they had replaced the card catalogue with a computer system. I felt stupid and was too ashamed to even ask for help. I find that truth silly today, but it was truly how I felt back then.

It was Rodney, the guy I was living with at the time, that decided he wanted to go back to college. I had never put much thought into college but decided I needed to learn about computers so when he applied, I applied.

I believe we went to some community college and took our entrance exams. After we got our scores back Rodney decided to not pursue college and was instead going to look for a job. When he put the paper down, I picked it up. I saw an advertisement for a college that offered a Computer Science Degree. I decided to go for it.

I began school that year and I loved it. I went to school from 6pm to 10 pm Monday through Friday. I loved it with the exception of one of my computer classes. I didn't understand any of it. Reading the book did not help. I felt as if it was written in another language. In a way it was; D.O.S. Back then windows had not even been invented. My computer final was going to be writing a menu system for the computers in the lab!

I literally went to bed crying after being in school for the first two weeks. I loved sociology and my other class as well but the computer class was taking me down. I was failing. I had never failed at anything. I found myself crying at the end of my bed feeling like a total loser. I could not get a job without knowing how to use a computer and it looked like I was never going to master that skill. I know I prayed to God that night but I am not sure of what all I said to Him.

What I do know is this, when I went to class that next day, I understood everything. I ended up ruining the curve because I never scored less than a 98% in that class after that day. It was like knowledge was downloaded right into my head. I had total understanding to the point that I even caught something my teacher had missed when it came to the computers in the lab. Not all of them had CAD so when writing the menu system no one knew what computer they would be assigned to. In your program you had to have an error code and a redirect back to the menu written in for the computers that were without CAD.

Needless to say, I found myself on the Deans list. The college loved me so much they helped me get a job and helped me apply for a scholarship to the Women's Business Association or something like that. I won the scholarship. I was one of five girls to be awarded it in the state.

Due to life circumstances, I was forced to drop out of college before I got my degree but I had learned enough to land a job.

It does not surprise me when I read the bible and it tells me wisdom comes from God. I know this to be true. I went from feeling like DOS was another language to being able to understand it completely over night.

I still struggle when it comes to things in the computer world. I openly admit I am the worst Googler in the world. It takes me forever and a day to get something on my own. Now I go straight to prayer on the subject.

God taught me something else about praying for knowledge. Sometimes, the timing is not right and the knowledge will remain hidden. I prayed off and on for over a year to be able to know how to write an e-book and self publish. I knew in my heart it was how I was going to do things. I would pray and then I would seek but nothing.

When it was time for me to write my first book, I knew it was time. I can't explain that feeling but I'm sure you have had it at least once yourself. A pull at your heart that makes you want to move even when you are not ready and you have not the slightest idea how to go about it. That was how writing these books happened for me.

For an entire year, I talked about wanting to write a book. I would ask those who had gone before me and they would point off to a direction that I simply could not wrap my brain around. One girl was kind enough to tell me to use smashwords. I laugh about it now because when she advised me to use smashwords I thought it was some type of typing program that would smash my words the right way for an e-book. It was months later when I felt that tug that I sought and stumbled upon a smashwords You Tube video! Here I am with God's help on book three.

It is six thirty in the morning and I have completed another one of my 'Only God could have done that' stories.

I love how He moves me and allows me to get things done. Mike started a new job and has to leave the house by 5:30 AM. This allows me two full hours in the morning all to myself in a home with 5 sleeping children. This morning I drank my protein, fiber, and greens shake, took a shower, moved laundry, unloaded the dishwasher, made a cup of coffee and shared a moment in time all in an hour and a half!

God gives you what you need when you need it. Our problem is often we confuse our wants with needs. This reminds me of a story in the bible. It is in both Luke and Matthew, but I will take it from Luke. For those of you who are curious about Jesus and his three-year ministry, I would encourage you to follow the story as told by Luke for he writes it all in chronological order. I did a one-year study through Luke and found myself a believer of Christ.

When you see how it reads and you have a teacher that points out the messianic miracles performed and ties it all together I don't think you can become anything other than a devout believer in Christ. That is how it happened for me anyway. I don't pretend to have all the answers about God I just have an unshakeable faith today.

A story as re-told by Luke, Chapter 11, verses 11:13:

> Verse 11: Which of you fathers, if your son asks for a fish, will give him a snake instead?
>
> Verse 12: Or if he asks for an egg, will give him a scorpion?
>
> Verse 13: If you then, though you are evil, know how to give good gifts to your children, how much more will your Father in heaven give the Holy Spirit to those who ask Him!" (Luke 11:11-13, NASB)

I think many times we confuse who is giving us what. The evil one came to steal, kill and destroy. Jesus came so that we could have life and live it abundantly. This life is full of hard knocks as well as brutal kicks to the mouth.

You can go a long way when you are living in your own strength depending on how determined you are It will be a climb and it will not be easy. However, when you give your life to God, even in the midst of a spiritual battle, you will find rest. I much prefer living my life this way.

I have a very strong will. I have always been determined to live my life my way. It took me a darn long time to get on my knees and tell God I was done and ready to live His will and give up mine.

It is now 6:45 A.M. I have enough time to pamper myself so pamper I am going to do! I am one chapter closer to finishing this third book and I love how I told God I needed big signs and a lot of help right now and as He is always Faithful, He is delivering in multiple ways. He is my Father and He loves me. He feels the same way about you. Until the next chapter, be blessed and be a blessing.

Wendy, Walks with God, Mom of Many

PS: I wrote this chapter right before my old lap top died and right before I enrolled myself back into college. This time I am studying first for an associate's degree in biblical studies. I have no idea what is next but I start my first online class in July of this year. I am excited for I truly believe this is where God intends me to be. It's incredibly exciting to feel confident that you are walking in the Spirit. I know if I struggle with any class the Lord is the provider of wisdom. If He would grant my heartfelt plea for understanding regarding something like computer science, then He will give me all the wisdom I can hold on to as I need it. I just find it all very cool. Faith is where it's at!

** Side note, I have now completed 12 courses. I am more than half way to earning my degree in Biblical Studies and God has indeed helped me along the way!

Father I thank you for all you have opened before my eyes. I know I am blessed in my seeking of you. I thank you for my abundant life. Today I pray that all those seeking you do so with all their heart and I pray they have enough belief to begin to see you working in their life so that their faith and belief and joy grow and grow. I pray they lean on you and trust you in the midst of all storms. I pray they read your word, learn the truth about Christ and then share the good news. In Jesus name I pray. Amen.

Wendy, walks with God,

Mom of Many

Chapter 3

How Delightful Delilah Came to Be

By the time I found myself pregnant with Delilah, it was the 11th time I had been blessed with a baby. Like other times, I knew I was pregnant with her as soon as she was conceived. Mike claimed I was paranoid. However, I just knew I was pregnant. Somewhere in the back of my head I was remembering what God had promised me. I was going to be a mother to many.

I knew while many may consider how Delilah had come to be an accident, that in Gods eyes she was no accident. He was showing His power to me. To my very core I know He was showing me in His own way that He was faithful in His promises.

I have often felt guilty for not wanting all the children God blessed me with. Especially as I have met women who wanted their own child and were unable to conceive.

The guilt weighed in on me even harder as I came back to God longing for the relationship I had had with Him as a child. I truly felt my decision to end two lives would forever keep me separated from Him.

When I had proof that I was pregnant with another baby and in knowing that becoming pregnant with her should have never even been an option, I knew God was showing me that I still had a little bit of His favor.

I say Delilah should have never been conceived not just because I was using birth control when she was conceived. No, it is much bigger than that which is why her conception is in this book.

The conception of Delilah is an absolute wonder for the

opportunity for her to be conceived should have never come to pass.

You see, exactly one month prior to Michael being born, Mike's father passed away. Not his biological father, Larry, the man who had raised Mike since he was three years old, was the one that passed away.

His passing was very hard on Mike. Larry and he had always been close until Mike had gone to prison. That had altered their relationship somewhat due to the fact that Larry had decided that Mike did not deserve to see his first born son again.

When Mike and I ended up getting together and I ended up pregnant with the twins that had altered their relationship in a more destructive way.

When Larry passed away, Mike and he were in the midst of a deep drift in their relationship and I know that had killed Mike.

I think he was left with anger and a realization that he was not going to get the chance to speak his mind or to repair what had been damaged.

If that was not enough to weigh on Mike's heart, my oldest son lost his first baby. She was only 3 months old and when she passed, my son was helping Mike out of a jam.

I think Mike believed had he not taken my son away from his baby that night, his daughter may never have died.

The guilt ate at him and in a way I lost Mike during the summer of 2006. We barely saw each other. He left early for work and often returned late. He was drinking a lot.

One fateful night, he had gone out to go 4 wheel driving out on River Road. About the time he had promised to be back at home, my phone rang. When I answered it, I quickly realized it was Mike that was yelling into my phone. I could hear loud music as if he was in a bar or at some kind of party. I asked him, "Where are you?"

"I'm at a concert. I got a free ticket. Can you hear the music? WooooooHooooooooo!" he screamed into the phone. He was ecstatic. I was not.

Since he couldn't hear me on the other end, I hung up the phone. He was obviously drinking and that meant to get home he was going to be drinking and driving.

It was around July 4th and as I had come to learn, July 4th was not a good time for Mike. Trouble seemed to come looking for him during that particular time of year.

Sure enough midnight rolled around and Mike had not returned home. I had called his phone only to have it go straight to voicemail. I went to bed knowing I would get a call when I would get a call.

Around 6 in the morning, my phone rang. Mike asked me to take the $900 he had given me to put back the night before and come bail him out of jail. He had indeed been arrested for drinking and driving. There is a crazy story outside of the Delilah story regarding this particular arrest, but this is not the book for it.

Within two weeks of Mike's first arrest, he was arrested for drinking and driving again. As many who have been through the court system know, it is a process. It took almost a year for Mike to go to court and finally be sentenced for his two offenses.

His lawyer managed to get them both tried in a way that Mike walked away with as little time as a person could get for such charges. He was sentenced to 90 days in jail and 90 days on

166

house arrest. In Indiana, you actually serve half the time you are sentenced to behind bars. The time on house arrest is day for day.

The day we went to court, the judge allowed Mike the rest of the day to get his affairs in order before he turned himself in to serve his 45 days. Within a couple of days of Mike going to jail, he had called me sharing how he was studying the bible with a group of guys and was loving what he was learning. I began checking out the bible myself. At the time I was simply looking at the Lord's prayer in the gospels and I was comparing how it was written within each account. My curiosity for God's word was just being peaked.

It was when Mike first went to jail that I began hanging out with my little sister who had just moved back into town. She and I somehow had gotten on the subject of birth control and how so many of them had failed me. It was then that she excitedly told me about these new condoms that were made out of lambskin. She even bought me a pack of them so Mike and I could see if we preferred them over the chemical inserts we were using at the time.

Mike had been locked up for only 13 days when I received a collect phone call from him telling me to be at the jail at midnight because he was being released one minute after midnight.

When he told me the news, I asked, "How can that be?"

"I don't know." He replied. "Someone messed up the paper work. I even told them as much but they insist I am going to be released after midnight. They will probably figure it out but just in case, I need you here to pick me up."

My babysitter at the time agreed to keep the children over night so that I didn't have to drag them out of bed in the middle of the night.

I arrived as requested at midnight. At about 2 AM I watched Mike come out of the jail and run to the car. I could not believe my eyes. He was supposed to serve 45 days straight and somehow, they had not gotten the paper work at the jail to hold him for the thirty days of jail time he had been sentenced with for his second offense. They had only received the paperwork for the first offense which had him serving 30 days do 15 with a credit for one day served.

At that time, 13 days was the longest Mike and I had been apart. When we got home, I showed him the gift Cady had given me and we gave it a try.

We have never used lambskin condoms again. The first one we used didn't hold up and I found myself with child.

As soon as I knew for sure I was pregnant, I could not deny that this baby was a gift from God. While she may have seemed like an accident to all who heard how she had been conceived, she was no accident in my eyes.

I truly believe God let Mike out of jail just so Delilah could be formed in my womb according to His timing. I am sure He loved showing me He was active where my life was concerned.

Travis was 5 years old at the time and he was going to kindergarten half day. The second half of the day, he traveled with me while I ran sales calls.

When I had my ultrasound and discovered I was carrying a girl, Travis insisted that we call her Delilah so he could sing the song, 'Hey there Delilah' to her. I was so touched that he wanted to sing to her that I decided I had to name her Delilah.

When I told my father I was carrying a girl, he suggested that we call her Valerie. When I put the two names together I did not like the way they sounded. Not to mention, I look at names in multiple ways trying to decipher all the ways a child can be made fun of for their name. I decided that naming a girl with the initials V.D. was not going to be a good thing.

She was due in January and by the time Christmas had arrived, my baby girl's name was still not set in stone.

It was while I was at my Grandma's house on Christmas day that my grandma asked me what I was going to name her. When I explained my dilemma, my grandma looked at me and asked, "When are you going to name a girl after me?"

I answered, "I named Amanda and Tia after you."

She replied, "You used Rose. You have not named a girl Rosemary yet."

That is when I came up with Valerie Rosemary Delilah. Soon after she was born she was nicknamed Delightful Delilah because she was such a delight to be around. I truly saw her for the gift she was. Through her, I knew God had not forgotten me. I was still not sure of how I would completely win His heart again, but I knew beyond a shadow of a doubt He had not forgotten about me!

I pray that you see that just like in the bible, God is faithful. He told me as a child that I would be a mother to many. All in all, He blessed me with 12 babies. I did not joyfully accept all of the blessings He gave me, but He continued to give them to me as He had planned all along. Even when my life was going in a way that it made it impossible for me to conceive a child, He made it happen by opening the prison gates and allowing Mike to walk out of prison just so Delilah could be formed when God intended for her to be.

This Sunday at church the teacher was talking about how God delighted in Adam when He created him. The entire discussion today was about God's nature and how again and again we are shown that He is both loving and compassionate, extending us grace even when we are the least deserving of it.

I smiled as we were informed that God took delight in us for I could not help but think of the delight I took in Delilah, one of the blessings God had given me.

I pray that you recognize the beauty in this particular story. God is truly magnificent. I am blessed that I sought Him as a child for I built a great relationship with Him. It was in my own foolishness that I ended that relationship. Even when I turned my back on God, He did not turn His back on me.

I know I have said it multiple times but that only proves it is true. I am blessed beyond measure in my seeking and I am truly thankful for that.

It is my prayer that you too come to understand you can have an amazing relationship with your heavenly Father. You just have to invest the time to get to know Him. Trust me when I say, He already knows you!

I encourage you to seek His word. Talk to Him every day. Find a radio station that sings praises and shares uplifting programs that inspire you and help to renew your mind as we are told to do in Roman's, Chapter 12, 1-3:

Verse 1: Therefore, I urge you brethren, by the mercies of God, to present your bodies a living and holy sacrifice, acceptable to God, which is your spiritual service of worship.

Verse 2: And do not be conformed to this world, but be

transformed by the renewing of your mind so that you may prove what the will of God is, that which is good and acceptable and perfect.

Verse 3: For through the grace given to me I say to everyone among you not to think more highly of himself than he out to think; but to think so as to have sound judgment, as God has allotted to each a measure of faith. (Romans 12:1-3, NASB)

All of us are born with a measure of faith. We are also born with free will. We must be careful what we put into our minds. What goes in will come out in some form. It is simply human nature. In knowing that truth, are you not curious as to how you might be transformed by what you put into your mind on a daily basis?

> When you seek
> You shall find
> It all begins
> With the renewing of your mind!

I did not get to where I am today overnight. It took many events as well as much seeking to bring me to where I stand today. I promise my studies and seeking have been more than worth the effort I put forth.

In life, we must work for anything we long to gain. We do not build relationships with people without effort. How do you think you can have a relationship with the Lord when you refuse to truly give Him anytime out of your day?

For the next thirty days, I encourage you to set aside the first ten minutes of each day and spend them with God. Just talk to Him. I honestly do not believe it matters where you open the conversation. Should you be in complete doubt, admit it. Say something like:

"God, I am in complete doubt that you actively participate in my daily welfare. You could say I am blind to your involvement. I would truly like to experience what others say they experience. I would like to know you are present. I want to have faith. Your word promises you give each one of us a measure of it. I would like my faith strengthened. In Jesus name I pray."

Admittedly until I accepted Jesus as my savior, I did not pray in His name. I just prayed. Often I just talked to God. I just poured my heart out. This is where your relationship must begin. If you had a relationship but ended the relationship you had due to feeling that God had let you down, I encourage you to open the conversation with that. He already knows your heart; the only way you will ever learn His is to go start that conversation.

Wendy, walks with God, Mom of Many

Chapter 4

On My Knees

By the time I was pregnant with my 4th child, the ongoing joke was always directed towards me and my fertility. I would get statements like; have you figured out how that happens yet? Or do you know what causes this?

I am here to tell you that when God wants you to have a baby you are going to become pregnant. Now He also allows us free will. The Lord knows I took advantage of that more than once. I am sad to admit it, but it is a truth about me.

If someone were to ask me today what I'd change about my life, my answer would be this; I would have kept all the babies God gave to me.

With that being said, by the time I became pregnant with Jeffrey I was done having children. Carrying and birthing Delilah just about 'killed' me physically. I am not sure where I would have ended had my baby sister not stepped in and enforced me staying with her for the week after Delilah came and insisted that my father give me the time off work with pay!

Through each pregnancy, Mike didn't make life any easier. It was almost as if he became harder to live with each time our family grew. I know this was due to the fact that my attention was diverted even more so with each new addition.

Regardless, as always, the jokes came at my expense anytime we were around family and friends. "So are you done now?"

I would reply, "Yes. I think God and I have an understanding now. I've told him I just can't handle another pregnancy."

I don't know of another girl who has tried harder to NOT get pregnant than me. I have conceived babies while using condoms, birth control pills, and birth control inserts. That brings me to Jeffrey.

My step-mother decided she wanted to have my sister's children and my children over for the weekend. It was the first time Mike and I had had any alone time since almost the beginning. It's certainly the first time we had an entire weekend. The birth control we had been using was causing some issues and as directed we had picked an alternate birth control to use for the next two months. The one we switched to was an insert kind. I should have read the fact that it is only 97.9% effective! It was the one we were using when Jeffrey was conceived.

With having time to just dote on each other, dote we did. I felt pregnant instantly. I pushed that feeling aside and told myself I was being silly.

I began praying that night to NOT be pregnant. The time for my cycle to start came and went with no visit from 'Aunt Rose'.

My prayer became more pleading and I was informing God how another baby was going to be way more than I could handle.

I went to the store and bought a two pack of pregnancy tests. I was 5 days late and full of dread. I did not read the directions on the box. I just looked at the picture on the front. If there were two pink lines right next to each other, it meant I was pregnant.

I completed my end of the test and placed the tester in the sink and went into the kitchen to start dinner. I went back into the bathroom and was relieved to see two single pink lines one in the test window and one on the other side but not two together! Negative! I thought to myself. I reasoned that I was probably not starting because of my fear level over the possibility that I may

174

be pregnant. I still got on my knees that night and prayed to start. Four days passed and still no 'Aunt Rose'.

That evening after work, I was in the bathroom again praying. This time I was actually on my knees. I was crying and praying. It had dawned on me that my first test was likely positive. You see, I had taken the time to actually read the directions that came with the pregnancy test. It turned out that for the test to be positive, the two pink lines did not need to be next to each other. There just needed to be two of them; one in the control window and one on the result side.

As I knelt on the floor believing that God may answer me and perhaps change the results of my test, I began by informing God about the fact that I wasn't strong enough to add another child to my day let alone go through another pregnancy. I told Him I would live with my fate but reminded Him that He could, if it was within His will, take this baby and gift someone else. I told Him I would appreciate that. I admitted that I had already tried the other two options when it came to one being pregnant and I admitted I could not live with those choices ever again. In the midst of my pleading prayer I was shaken by His voice.

"Wendy! This baby is a Blessing! This is how you will put down your cigarettes. Get up off your knees. Your hands will be so busy you will never miss them."

His voice was so prominent and so matter of fact. I was given such an in-depth answer that at once I did get up off my knees and I stopped crying instantly. I was filled with such a peace and awe that mere words cannot give it justice. At a desperate moment in my life, I was on the cusp of joy. You can only find that kind of feeling next to God.

I grabbed the package and took the second test out and opened it. I already knew I was pregnant. God had told me the child inside of me was a blessing. I only took the second test because I needed proof to show Mike. When I came back into the bathroom, I was greeted with two pink lines again.

When Mike came home, he went straight to our room first without even saying hello. I caught him in the doorway as he was exiting back out. I had the test in my hand and as I showed it to him I said, "I'm pregnant."

He looked at me completely dead panned and said, "We are not keeping it."

I replied, "I don't know who 'we' is but as far as I'm concerned there is no choice." I spun and left him there. We did not talk about it or anything else that night.

The next day I wrote down all of our bills, not including basics like gas, cigarettes, groceries, health insurance, etc. and divided them in half. As I shared the list with Mike I said, "I'm not going to be able to stay in sales. I will be put back behind a desk. You are going to have to help out financially and this is what I need from you."

He actually laughed at me and told me I was crazy.

I stood my ground and insisted, "Mike, if you don't give me your half of the hard core bills, you can't live here anymore."

It was the biggest battle of wills we had had to date. I ended up bringing him into the office with my father who Mike looks up to and had him be the moderator.

My father was shocked to know that this was even a battle. It was a bigger battle than I thought it would ever be and it stayed a battle all the way until I walked out and left Mike.

Jeffrey has indeed been a blessing in more ways than I can count.

He fills my life with laughter and joy that I can't even put into words. My heart sings when he is around. When I look at Him I am reminded that God spoke to me directly.

I did put the cigarettes down as I had been told I would. I quit with no trouble at all. My last cigarette was smoked at 10 PM the night before I was induced with Jeffrey.

My hands were indeed too busy and I never implemented a cigarette into my new routine. I thank God for taking that vice out of me even more so every time I see or hear about someone who is struggling with any kind of addiction.

Mike knows that at one point in my life I had decided to pray to a moon goddess I had read about in some book. Supposedly she would help you with being able to walk away from habits you wanted to be rid of. I wanted my prayer to her to work so badly that I actually did not smoke cigarettes again until the twins were born. I did sneak a puff off of one of Mike's cigarettes once when I was pregnant with the twins but they did not grab me like mine and I could not justify buying a pack of my own at the time.

I began smoking again while we were living in Colorado. One-night Mike was looking for a fight. He had run into his first love and he truly wanted a reason to justify being with her. He confessed to something he had done the day the twins were born.

Outside of giving Amanda up for adoption, my heart had never been punched so hard. As he gave me the details of the night, I found myself having trouble breathing. Maybe that is why I felt the need to breathe in toxic air. Plain air had no way of robbing one of feeling for even a single second.

I decided to go with Mike's brand due to the cost of pre-rolled cigarettes. At the time you could buy a pack of tops for only $1.49 and you got 36 cigarettes in each pack! I share all of this within this story for a couple of reasons The first one being when Mike found out I was worshipping a moon goddess over The Most High God, he literally blanched in front of me and warned me about how much that angered God. He actually told me he was worried about me because of my praying to anyone outside of God.

He was the first man I had ever been with that showed true heart when it came to the importance of not putting anyone above God. I was intrigued to say the least.

I had only prayed to this goddess because I believed God did not have time to concern Himself with the likes of me anymore. I thought of Him as only a punishing God and I was tired of my life and its never ending troubles. I was looking for a higher power that claimed to be able to do tricks for me if I were to pray in a certain way with certain props at a certain time of the moon cycle.

I laugh and shake my head now that I have been un-blinded and fully see that God and God alone is the one who can answer prayers.

When I first told people about me being on my knees praying and what I had heard, I always felt weird about adding the cigarette detail but it was truly a part of what was said to me so I knew I could not leave it out.

It was in the retelling of my story for this book that I understood what else God wanted me to share; He is the one we pray to. He is the one we worship. He is the One we sing praises to and give thanks to. Not some false god or goddess. He is the only one that can remove afflictions permanently. He removed that vice from me because He saw in my heart that I truly wanted to be rid of it. In other words, He gave me the desires of my heart even though I had not gone to Him in prayer regarding such things.

My prayer for anyone reading this book is this: May you build a relationship with our heavenly Father. May you begin reading His word and believing in what you read. May the words make sense to you.

Blessing to all who are willing to try,

Wendy, walks with God, Mom of Many

Chapter 5

Saved by an Army of Angels

My son Michael is the child I wrote about in my blog titled "Who do You Curse, Why Do You Curse Them?"

He was born on November 21, 2005. The event that you are about to read took place right after his fourth birthday. It was the weekend after Thanksgiving. I was approximately 20 weeks pregnant at the time with my last child Jeffrey. Mike was helping a friend with some yard work and I was home with the fantastic four. We had been having a great day. We were watching movies and doing laundry when literally all hell broke loose.

Michael was my little strong man at the time so he had a lot of trust built up with me. I was beginning to have trouble with moving. At this point, Mike and I were hardly talking. He was hateful to me and showed no sympathy at all regarding to how hard this pregnancy was on me. He purposely gave me no room on our bed so that I would either be forced to beg for more room or I could lay on my right side night after night weeping myself to sleep. I never let Mike see me crying. I just felt so unloved and confused by him that I wept a lot. It truly broke my heart that he had no love to share with me. That is not to say we did not have relations. We did. However, sex without love is empty.

I think it was due to me sleeping on one side night after night that my back and hips were in so much pain. Due to this pain, Michael ended up being the one to help me drag things like laundry baskets around for me.

So in the midst of him helping me with such tasks, he was sidetracked by my lighter. I was still smoking cigarettes at this time. Over the summer, his father had taught him how to set camp fires and his older brother had taught him how to actually light a lighter. Michael was fascinated by the flame and had already set a couple of little fires outside. He had been warned that making fires without an adult was not wise. Never in a million years did I see what was about to happen.

You see, Michael had grabbed my lighter in the midst of doing our chores. He was supposed to be grabbing a laundry basket out of my closet and bringing it to the garage.

Instead, he had found a lighter and had decided to climb up on his sister's loft bed above the twins' bed. Tia always had loose paper at the head of her bed. I had built her headboard as a cabinet so she could keep paper and books up on her bed where no one else was supposed to be.

That turned out to be not such a great idea. Michael knew there was paper stored up on Tia's bed and that was why he had climbed up there. He set a piece of Tia's school papers on fire.

Marie and Marissa had gone to look for Michael and it was Marissa that came running to tell me that the bed was on fire. I rushed into the hall and saw the flames. At first I ran to the room and that is when I quickly realized that this fire was already too big to deal with without the help of water.

I ran to the kitchen and for the life of me, I couldn't find anything bigger than a punch bowl for water. My heart was racing. I frantically scanned the kitchen and saw the trash can. I grabbed the liner out of it and ran down the hallway with the trash can and dashed into the bathroom and began filling it with water.

We are on a well and I am here to tell you that day our pressure seemed to be nothing more than a trickle. I looked out into the hallway toward the bedroom and to my horror realized the fire seemed to have tripled in a matter of seconds. I glanced back toward the kitchen and all the kids were standing at the end of the hallway with terror in their eyes.

I rushed them all out the back door and closed it telling them to stay outside. I ran back to the bathroom grabbed what water was in the can and ran to the room. The fire was already on the bottom bunk bed. Because of that, I couldn't stand on it to get the water onto the loft bed. I threw all the water on the bottom bed. I knew my only shot at putting out this fire was going to be the garden hose.

I ran outside to grab it. My only available hose was a junk one that kinked with ease. I had spent money on a really nice one at the beginning of the summer for my kid toys but Mike had accidentally burnt it in half over our burn pit approximately two months prior to this event.

He had no remorse regarding the destruction of the hose and refused to help purchase a new one so in my spite I had replaced it with the cheapest one I could buy. When I went to grab it, it was not convenient.

Mike had used it last and it was stretched out over the yard and wrapped around the patio table and under a couple of chairs. My heart lurched.

Michael went right into action and helped me unwind it like a pro. I never saw a kid move so fast. I had him turn the water on full blast as I ran into the house with it. Much to my disbelief the hose was 3 feet short of being able to get any spray to the biggest part of the fire.

I knew to reach the fire I would have to bring it in through my bedroom window. It was my only hope. I tore through the plastic I had just put up the weekend before and with the strength of God,

I managed to get the storm window up.

Our home was filling with smoke. I leaned out the window as far as I could and caught a good breath of air. As I ran past my door I hit the light switch turning off my ceiling fan as I was instructed to do by someone I could not see (an angel is my personal belief).

I ran back out of the house with the hose. I rushed to my window and shoved the hose through it. I yelled at the kids to go to the van and I ran back into the house closing the door behind me. I no sooner rounded the corner when I found myself in a total cloud of black smoke. I was literally choked out and I remember falling to the floor.

The next thing I remember is being given a breath of fresh air and hearing. "Wendy stay low. People die in fires."

I sped crawled to the hose and yanked it into the girls' room and began fighting that fire on my knees. This may sound crazy to you but I was not in that room alone. God sent an army of angels to help me. The things I did over the course of the next few minutes were nothing less than miraculous. I am sure my training fighting fires when I was a child helped me with my performance, but many of the things I did, I did because I was TOLD to do them.

I watched in horror as the fire leapt across the ceiling to the other side of the room. I heard it try to get around me before I even saw it. No sooner had I gotten the room under control when I heard "Go soak the roof."

I ran into my room and threw the hose out of my window. I then ran outside and pulled the hose through my window and began

soaking down the roof. Within a couple of minutes, I was told to go back inside. I ran by my window and threw the hose in it again. This time when I went back in, you couldn't see a thing due to all the black smoke in the house. I think it was the first time in my life I was grateful for being legally blind. I ran in holding my breath and when I hit the hallway, I slid on my knees as far as I could go. I found the hose again and finished putting the fire out.

It was so hot in the house, I feared the fire might be burning behind the walls. I was on my way out the front door when I heard "Turn off the power". I stopped at the entry way and then I ran into the garage and flipped the main breaker off. I ran out the garage door got in the van and made sure everyone buckled up.

I drove to the fire station because I had no phone to call for help. Their door was locked. I couldn't see anyone through the window, so I began banging on the door and screaming for help. I hit the garage doors. I banged on the people door. Finally, a couple of fire fighters came to the door. I stammered, "My house, it was on fire. I think I put it out but I'm not sure I got it completely out. I need help."

The look on their faces is something I'll never forget. They were dumbstruck is the best way to explain it. One of them said, "Mam, are you okay? You have soot all over your face."

I looked at her and screamed, "I WAS IN THE FIRE!"

They looked over my shoulder at the van and said, "You have children with you?"

I said, "Yes, they are okay they weren't in the fire. Please, I need you to go to my home and see if it's still burning."

I quickly told them where I lived and off they went. One of the firefighters came to the van to look at the children and she grabbed some blankets for me since we'd all run out without coats or even shoes. She asked if I had anyone I'd like to call. I told her my dad. I don't even remember what I told him but he was there in mere moments.

He had me follow him down to the road west of my driveway and from there we watched the firemen walking up and down my driveway.

I asked my dad to sit with the kids so that I could find out what was going on. As I was walking up the driveway an older firefighter was walking back towards the road.

I walked up to him and asked, "Was it still burning?"

He stopped, looked at me and said, "No. You got it all out."

I said, "I wasn't sure. It was so hot and there was so much steam. It looked like smoke was coming out of the walls."

He stared at me for a second then shook his head and said, "Do me a favor. Next time run. I don't know how you fought this fire, but don't ever do something like that again."

I continued on down the drive to my home knowing I fought this fire with an Army of Angels. God had saved me, my family and my home.

As I approached my stepping stones, I was stopped by another man who turned out to be the Assistant Fire Marshall. He informed me that what he had found indicated that my son was abused and obviously hated his older sister. I was not only shocked, I was insulted.

The police showed up and questioned me and the Assistant Fire Marshall informed me that the department of children services would be in touch. He also told me that since it was of his opinion that my son who set the fire was an abused child, I was

185

being ordered to have to take him in for an evaluation at a mental facility.

My whole world was spinning. Abused child? None of my children were abused I told him.

Even my father was stunned by this man's approach. He stuck to his opinion. He informed me that children didn't set fires unless they were angry and abused.

Again I told him he was misinformed. Regardless, it did not matter. Firemen are just another arm of the law and you must abide by their rules.

He made an appointment for me with a place that deals with adolescents. I was terrified. Michael had just turned four and he was going to have to be interviewed. From this they would decide whether or not I got to keep him and the rest of my children.

I am happy to say that the doctor that interviewed him found him to be a normal child. She was a little upset when I explained that I did not believe he had any anger issues. She looked at me and asked, "Do you mean to tell me the only reason you are here is because the fire department insisted on you bringing him?"

I explained everything. She abruptly stood up and said, "I'll be right back." She left Michael and me in the room. She came back in about 10 minutes and informed me that we were done and sent us on our way. The Department of Children Services never contacted me over this incident.

The children that were present with me that day will tell you that an army of angels saved me. I did not know until a year later that those kids had watched their room burn from the outside bedroom window. I discovered that they thought I was going to die in the house.

It was what Michael said in the interview with that lady that gave me understanding in what had happened. He told her that fires can get big! He was harder to understand back then so she had asked him to repeat what he had said again. He told her he tried to punch the fire out but it just got bigger and bigger. I realized that he had sent sparks all over Tia's bed by trying to smack the fire out. It suddenly made much more sense to me.

I was thankful to have lived through the fire and thankful the ordeal with the hospital was behind me.

If you had seen the hose that I fought the fire with you would have to admit that me putting out a 3 alarm fire with that thing was nothing short of a miracle.

As long as I live I'll never forget being filled with a breath of fresh air. Nor will I forget being advised on what to do to put out the fire itself. Had I not gone out and watered down the roof, the fire would have gone through it. When we tore out the insulation you could see the fire had scorched the roof and was mere seconds from getting all the fresh air it needed to consume the entire home.

I coughed up black tar from my lungs for over a week. Everything smelled like a musty camp fire for days.

Mike blamed me for the fire. It broke my heart that he had no compassion at all for what I'd been through. He had come hometo find it burnt and no one there. He called my father figuring he would know something. When he came to my dad's house, he didn't even hug or kiss me. He didn't give thanks for us all being alive. He was upset that he had to be the one to tear out all the burnt walls, ceiling and insulation as well as clean up and repair our home.

On top of everything he said and the hateful way he acted, he informed me that I was not a good enough parent. He insulted me on multiple levels. It was not a good time for us.

I don't know why God felt the need to save me that day. I am just grateful He did.

I hope this chapter gives you cause to be amazed. It is my prayer that reading my story will encourage you to get into God's Word.

He is using me, a murderer of unborn children to show you that anyone that leans on Him and believes in Him can make it into the Kingdom of Heaven. All you have to do is find your Faith. I have been a BIG sinner over the course of my life and yet God still loves me. I committed the ultimate sin of killing unborn babies. Not just one baby but two. ANYONE can be saved. You are required only one thing. Belief that Jesus bore the cross for ALL. I pray that my story helps you with this.

Blessings to All who read this and believe,

Wendy, walks with God, Mom of Many

Chapter 6

Awoken by an Answer to a Prayer!

This by far is one of the strangest things I have ever witnessed. Allow me to paint the scene.

Jeffrey Thomas was born. He came to work with me every day like many of my babies have. I breast feed the majority of my children and having your baby with you is much more pleasant than having to pump! Anyway, at this time my mother was my assistant at work. She always came by the house to allow me to get to work on time and she would stay with the other children to get them on the school bus.

One morning when she showed up I immediately realized something was wrong with her face. In a panic I called my father and told him what was going on. My brother was sent to my house and he rushed my mom to the emergency room. I thought she was having a stroke.

Up until that point I had never heard of an illness known as Bells Palsy. If you have yourself never heard of it, the symptoms are a lot like a stroke. My mom had lost use of one side of her face.

The hospital informed her there is no cure. They prescribed blood pressure medicine and antibiotics.

The most awful thing about this disease is it leaves you with no control over one side of your face.

My mom has always been one of those people that pay attention to looks. How pretty, how thin, these things matter to her.

I know looking in the mirror was too much for her. I cannot

fathom what it would be like to not be able to close your eye or to smile on both sides of your face. My heart broke for her.

After a few days of antibiotics and no change I was on my knees praying for God to heal her. I told Him this, "I need my mom. If this paralysis of her face doesn't improve I think she will go insane. Please God, you have to heal her. You have to. Thank you in advance." and I went to bed.

That morning I awoke to this reply, "Put your breast milk in your mother's ear."

I sat straight up in bed. I was taken aback. Shocked. Perplexed. Confused. Worried on how to even approach the matter. I was in such a state of fear that I didn't even say anything at first. I spent the first 4 hours of my day searching the Internet for Bells Palsy information.

Somehow I stumbled upon an article regarding the 7th cranial nerve as this is the one responsible for the face having movement. I then spent another hour researching the 7th cranial nerve and that is when I found the picture of a baby's ear. Ironically, it showed the 7th cranial nerve and how it travels through the ear. Now I was stunned because I knew in my heart I had to approach the subject.

With a moment of courage, I spun my chair around and said, "Mom, this is going to sound so crazy but I went to bed praying for you to be healed by God and this morning I was awoken by a message. I was told to put some of my breast milk in your ear." Then I showed her the diagram I had found of the 7th cranial nerve and asked her how she felt about us trying that.

She looked at me and said, "Wendy, I'm willing to try anything at this point. I just want to be able to shut my eye."

I went into the bathroom and pumped out some milk. Luckily, since I have raised children here in the office, I even had a medicine dropper handy. I soaked up some of my milk into the dropper and dripped it into her ear. I sat down and within a minute she kind of jumped in her chair and said, "I felt something pop." and then she blinked her eye. Next she moved her cheek slightly.

Holding back my tears, I said, "I'm pumping some for you to take home and just put in drops every three hours over the weekend." I ran into the bathroom more to give thanks and to weep than to pump. I was overwhelmed with gratitude.

We couldn't get any doctors to take notice of what had transpired. After more research, I discovered there are laws against even sharing bodily fluids (such as breast milk). I am thankful that God heard my plea and gave me a solution. The joke in our family for a while was that I should bottle my breast milk and call it "miracle milk".

I realized what happened is even bigger than my milk curing my mom. I would have never thought of that on my own. Obviously so by my simple minded need to research endlessly regarding what I had heard.

Indeed, Jeffrey has been a blessing in many ways. Had I not given birth to him I would not have been lactating and there would not have been breast milk on hand to use in my mother's ear.

While all prayers aren't answered immediately and all of our loved ones are not miraculously healed please do not allow yourself to believe that for one-minute God doesn't feel for you or your loved ones. He sent his only begotten son to save us. This life span of ours is nothing more than a vapor. We are nothing more than a blimp when it comes to time. We all in the end face the same fate: bodily death. The bigger picture is this: eternal life.

My prayer for you if you are currently a non believer or one who has doubts when it comes to God is that you do your due diligence in educating yourself on your beliefs and how you came to form them.

I am currently reading a book titled *How Now Shall We Live,* written by Charles Colson and Nancy Pearcey. It covers evolution, naturalism along with many other kinds of science.

Science has actually has proven there is a single designer behind the curtain. Even the big bang theory leads the biggest atheist to the truth. God exists. Why is this being withheld from our science books in school? Why are we still teaching Darwinism?

Just like in the days of Jesus, many of our religious leaders have done a complete injustice to God. It is no wonder so many resist searching out God to begin with.

In a world of children killing children, perhaps it's something we, as parents, should at least be curious enough about to do some serious soul searching ourselves. I challenge all non believers to read the above mentioned book. It's not the Bible; however, it is a well thought out intellectual read.

My prayer for everyone today is that you take a moment of silence at the end of each day to question. Where did I come from? What is my purpose? What am I to teach my children about life? Blessings to all who take me up on this challenge.

Wendy, walks with God, Mom of Many

Chapter 7

Show Me a Sign

This actually happened to me on December 26, 2010. It is one of the things God urged me to share again. As his humble servant I have promised to listen to his direction! I hope this true story helps you with your faith!

Boy oh boy do I have a story to share! I am a real believer in not getting into debt. If I don't have the cash, I can't afford it. So I pay all of my bills in cash. This is why on December 26th, I was walking around with approximately $1300.00 in my wallet. It was all earmarked for bills that I needed to pay and a whopping $240 to play with that my kids and I had received from family for Christmas.

Now you should know in my house we don't put up a tree and do the whole Santa thing. I just really think the whole world has gone a little crazy in the Christmas area. So, we bake a cake and sing happy birthday to Jesus even though we know December 25 is not the day he was born.

I tell my kids that they need to pray to God to for wisdom, protection, and for kinder hearts. I tell them to ask for help when dealing with their brothers and sisters. I tell them they can also ask that He help me find things they have wished for throughout the year. I go to Goodwill's and Thrift stores to shop. With 7 kids in the house, it is honestly the only way I can afford to do anything special at all!

On a short list, I did find a Tonka remote control dump truck for Michael for $4.00 and a Fisher Price Digital Camera for Marissa for a whopping $3.00. I also found a Barbie computer learning game for Marie that was the exact same one her cousin had gotten the year before that Marie LOVED and had asked for about a million times priced at $2.99! For my littlest one and my two-year-old, I found some awesome toys all wonderfully priced. You know God loves his babies! Tia and Travis were just as lucky with items they had asked for. Goodwill is also the greatest place to buy books for kids and since we have what we call library time at night. I wanted some new kid books to read and boy oh boy did I score there!

After breakfast I asked who wanted to help me in the bonus room with laundry and of course everyone offered as they were still on their best behavior knowing that God was watching.

I had spread all the gifts out on the floor and as we walked out the door they were all overwhelmed with joy over the items God had led me to for them. Needless to say for the rest of the morning everyone was wonderful, sharing their toys, reading the books, taking pictures, and driving the dump truck. It was a truly pleasurable morning. I sipped on my coffee and smiled to myself as my kids all thanked God for helping me find what they had wanted.

From there we went to my Grandma's house and then off to my sister's house for the remainder of the day. Worn out and looking forward to a shopping trip to Value World on 52nd and Keystone where I had been blessed enough to score a 50% off coupon for the entire thrift store, the kids and I all fell into our beds and were fast asleep.

The next day around 11:00 AM we were officially on our way to go shopping. I had seen some bird cages at a local goodwill when I had gone shopping prior to Christmas. My Uncle Bob loves birds and I had asked if he'd be interested in these cages. He had said yes so we stopped there first. I grabbed the cages and then saw a high chair that was marked $10 but was also 50% off so I grabbed it.

Mike lost patience while standing in line and left me in the store with 5 children and a full cart along with the high chair.

This was a time in my life where my pain level was off the charts. Mike felt that he was doing me a favor by making me struggle. He claimed it kept me strong.

All I really longed for was him to help out more or for him to be gone. What good is a partner who doesn't do his part?

Anyway, my back was pretty bad and I was hurting something awful. I paid for our stuff and then fought my way out the store with the children, the highchair, and my cart. Mike was in the van waiting for us.

I was so mad I didn't trust myself to speak. I loaded the children and the items into the van while Mike watched me struggle. I climbed up into the passenger seat and requested we stop off at home first to unload all of our items.

When we got home he did help carry in the high chair at my request. I stopped him in the garage and said, "Look. I'm really bad today and I don't want to get angry with you. So, if you can't be a gentleman today, I'd rather you stay here."

He looked at me with this blank look. I continued, "Opening that side door on that van kills me. Having you walk off leaving me with everything makes me insanely angry. I don't want to be angry so if you can't do this for me today, it would be best for you to not join us."

He grinned at me and asked me to clarify what I wanted. I said this, "Every movie that you have ever seen where a man treats a lady like a lady, that's what I need from you today. If you can't do that then don't come."

He assured me he was capable of that. I tried calling Tia and Travis one more time as they were at their Grandmother's for Christmas morning but they were still not answering the phone. I told Mike I wanted to drive since I knew the best route to go and giving him directions usually ended up with me being upset.

We headed out and had made it to 80th and Keystone when Jeffrey, my youngest child was losing his mind. Mike suggested we pull over and switch drivers so I could tend to Jeffrey Thomas. When I pulled over, I got out and walked around to the side door of the van and waited for Mike to open the door from the inside. All of a sudden the side window rolled down and he yelled, "Are you going to get in or what?"

I can't even tell you the anger I felt in that moment. It took everything I had in me to get that door opened and then closed. I was so mad I was crying silently. He so didn't get it! No sooner than I got buckled in, Tia and Travis called. I had Mike head over to Allisonville to go back and get them. Not five minutes into our ride Mike began berating me over the amount of gas we had in the car.

Somehow I managed to calmly say, "Mike if the level of gas is a problem, pull into the next gas station and we can fill up."

Like most children do, when we pulled up to the pump, they all suddenly needed to go to the bathroom. I unloaded them and told Mike I'd pay inside. Once in the store, I reached into my coat to get my money out. That is when I realized I did not have my wallet on me anymore. I told myself even though I was already beginning to panic, it's in the console.

I ran to the van and asked Mike if my wallet was in the console. It was not. "What about on the floor." I suggested, "Maybe it

196

fell."

Again he said, "No."

I was sick. Every dime I had was in that wallet. I was crying pretty hard on the inside and praying to God silently to please help me.

I called the Goodwill I had gone to first to see if by chance I had left my wallet there. No. They did not have it but they did take down my number just in case someone found it and turned it in.

When we picked up Tia and Travis I told them the bad news.

Just as we were getting ready to turn around and back track our steps, my phone rang. Now, bear in mind, my cell number is listed on our voice mail message at work just encase someone needs something after hours so I was not sure who was calling. Even though the last thing in the world I wanted to do was talk about was fence, I answered my phone trying not to let on to the fact that I was crying. "Hello." I said as calmly as I could muster.

The voice on the other end asked if they could talk to Wendy.

I wasn't sure I could pull off a long conversation at the moment without giving away the fact that I was crying so I asked who was calling.

They said, "Well I am someone who might have found something she has lost."

I replied, "Oh my! Did you find my wallet!"

She said, "Yes and I can't wait to meet you."

We arranged a place to meet and described our cars to each other. (It turns out I had actually lost the wallet when we had pulled

197

over into an apartment complex on 80th street between Keystone Ave & Dean Rd to switch drivers so I could calm down the baby.)

When we arrived, I got out of the van. The most beautiful woman I had ever seen was standing there to greet me. She took my hands and said, "I have to bear witness to you."

She proceeded to tell me the unusual journey she had taken, completely out of her way, but led in that path by God's voice when she came upon my wallet. This angel of God had to look me up on the Internet and she found me through Glidden Fence!

The most amazing thing to me, is she gave me a direct answer to a prayer. There is NO way she could have known what I had been asking God for over the last six months. She told me as if it were no big deal, "Oh, God told me to tell you that you are one of his favorite people and to let you know not to worry, he has heard you. In me returning your wallet, you have your answer to your prayer."

Now, to many of you that most likely is vague, but to me, she was right. That message did answer my prayer. I could not have asked for a bigger sign. Just so you know, my prayer for the last six months had been. "God, I have failed at this relationship thing so many times. I have 5 children with Mike. I want these children to grow up with their father in their lives but I'm not sure I can continue with him. I need a sign. If I leave Mike will I be able to make it financially on my own?"

So, to all of those of you, who have questioned whether God is with us or not, I assure you He most definitely is!

Wendy, Mom of Many

Chapter 8

Give it to God and Let it Go

Some have asked me why I blog what I think? I tell them, "The Holy Spirit inside me guides me to do so." It really is that simple.

I have advised others to use their talents while I have hidden mine. Please don't think me grandstanding, but I believe I have a gift. A God given gift. We are meant to share those. Mine is NOT that I am a brilliant writer. No, rather I think mine is being able to write what I hear quickly! I had a really good grade in typing class.

A year ago, I had shared the song *Beautiful* by Carole King on my Face Book page. It had woken me up. I seriously thought one of the kids had gotten up and turned on the radio. It was as if they were having a little fun by continually turning the volume up.

This is also during the time in my life that I was in immense pain daily. It was all I could do to meditate myself to sleep. Often I would lay in bed for hours with tears streaming out of my eyes before I could fall asleep. It was on one of these nights that I found myself asking God why I had to hurt so badly. I wanted Him to tell me what I needed to do to have a better life.

The next morning, music was what woke me up. At first it was soft and it lulled me awake. I did not want to wake up yet. The music seemed to get a little louder and I heard more of the words. I still refused to open my eyes and was honestly hoping the child that was messing around with the radio in the living room would stop. Instead, it was as if a deep drum beat sounded off three times and the words repeated. I still did not get up. Again, that drum beat and the music got louder. It was the fourth time when I pulled myself out of bed and shuffled to the living room ready to give the child in the living room a piece of my mind.

You cannot imagine how confused I was when I walked into the living room and found it empty just as the drums beat again. The words were sung to me one more time as I froze in place looking at the radio that was not on. I could hear the music clearly but the source was not visible. I was so amazed.

I went back into the bedroom and woke Mike up. He hadn't heard any music. I explained what had happened and then I sang the words to him. He did not recognize the tune.

Convinced it was a song, I came to work and sang it to my dad and my uncle. Neither knew it. My dad said it should be a song. Oh how that makes me laugh.

Anyway, it was my uncle who suggested I go to You Tube and type in the lyrics. That morning this was the verse that played in my head again and again and again:

"You've got to get up every morning with a smile on your face and show the world all the love in your heart. People gonna treat you better you're gonna find yes you will that you're Beautiful as you FEEL!"

That day I searched for every version of that song I could find on You Tube. Not one of them came close to the Amazing instrumental version I had heard sung by what I was now referring to as the Angel Band.

A little more than a year later, I found myself unable to stop worrying about an awful rumor a girl had started about me. Even though her lies held no truth, I could not stop my mind from worrying about it all.

I had set up a table at a small town event for my health and wellness business. This girl came up to my booth and I had asked her if she'd ever heard of my company. When she said no, I gave her my little spiel.

She told me she wasn't really interested because she cleaned her home with vinegar and made her own laundry detergent.

I have heard this more than once, so I also shared the nutritional food aisle and the first aid aisles with her. I told her I would love to share the store with her and if she was interested great and if not, no big deal.

She declined and walked away. Two other girls from other booths came over to my booth as there was no other customers walking through at the moment. The event as a whole had been a flop. We were all talking and I happened to glance over at the door and discovered this girl looking at me. I smiled at her and we continued talking about what a flop this event was and how I thought I wasn't going to do the next one even though I had paid for it and knew I wouldn't get my money back.

When I wrote the events coordinator to let her know I would not be present at the last event, she informed me of the ongoing situation. I was confused as to whom I could have offended and she kindly sent me a link to see for myself.

When I read the town thread, I was horrified. This lady had the audacity to say she felt like I had looked down my nose at her because she looked like a young mother. She claimed to be in her thirties. She credited me for words I would have never uttered. Her claims were so far beyond slander I had to calm myself before responding to the coordinator who had kindly informed me this lady was her personal friend.

After I collected myself, I wrote her back saying that if this lady was indeed a friend she needed to tell her to stop telling outright lies immediately. I informed her I was a teen mom and I would have never in a million years made such derogatory comments. I also warned her that if her friend intended on continuing her claims, I would be forced to hire an attorney. As far as those two were concerned, it was over.

Where I was concerned, it wouldn't leave my mind. I could not stop obsessing over what this girl had said about me. My name was associated with the lie as well as my company.

I got on my knees that night and prayed for God to remove it. In a gist I said, "God, I know this is nothing but I cannot stop myself from thinking about it continually. Please keep me from worrying about it."

The next morning, I was awoken to another instrumental song. "Free your mind and the rest will follow!" That was it. Just once. Loud and clear. I actually sat up in bed and laughed. I knew it was not a radio playing in the other room for we were in our RV camping when I heard it.

That day, I'll admit I thought about that girl and the nasty things she had said multiple times. Every time my focus turned to her, the music played and again I was told "Free your mind and the rest will follow!" It was about the fifth time it happened that I burst out in laughter and honestly haven't thought about that girl other than to share this story with others.

It makes me laugh that God chose songs to answer these two prayers. Through songs is often how I communicate best with my children when I want them to "get" something without an attitude.

I imagine the answer God gave me for these prayers is the same answer He would give all his children. He has never failed me and the better you get to know me. The more of my story you learn. The more you will realize and understand even those that believe in God will go through trials and tribulations. We all have days that are nuts. Just because I share my faith that God loves me does not mean I don't live a regular Joe Shoe life.

My prayer for you today is that you see the Glory of God for yourself.

May Your day be full of blessings.
May Your Joy over flow.
Whatever is troubling you today
Give it to God and let it go!

Wendy, walks with God, Mom of Many!

Chapter 9

How I Found Moody Radio!

When we rolled back into Indiana after having been gone for almost two full years, we were driving a mini-van that had a lot of problems. We knew we were going to have to replace our van soon and I was looking desperately for a replacement vehicle.

At the time, Mike and I had the twins and Michael. Tia and Travis spent every other week with me.

Within a week of arriving into town, Mike found a job on a tree farm. Within a few weeks there, they told him if he could find a truck and a couple good hands, he could become a subcontractor.

At the time, my Uncle Bob had my grandfather's truck for sale. It was a Ford F350 extended cab that was just what we needed. Without a true penny to our names, my Uncle Bob agreed to sell it to Mike and me for no money down. We turned around and paid him off the next month. It felt great.

I was one of Mike's helpers at first and I recruited Lena, my aunt, because she is one of the hardest workers I have ever had the pleasure of working side by side with.

After we paid off the truck, I thought Mike would begin to give me part of the earnings. A paycheck of sorts per say. When payday came that next week, he paid Lena and then he counted out $300 and give it to our baby sitter. He then informed me that my money went to pay the sitter. I was without a paycheck but did not throw a fit while everyone was still there. When they all left I let Mike know how I felt about what he had done but it was like I was talking to a wall.

Mike's boss could not figure out how Mike, with a crew of only two girls, could get so much done in a day. Lena and I were hard workers. He ended up hiring another person instead of taking my advice on purchasing a piece of equipment and within a couple more weeks of not getting paid, I quit.

With me not working, I had only my back child support rolling in for my own spending money. Mike ran his business and he controlled the money. He would give me money for groceries every week. I always shopped on a budget making the most of it. With the extra I would go to goodwill or garage sales to find awesome deals on clothes, shoes and toys.

One day, Mike came home extremely excited about a vehicle he had found. It was right in Westfield where we lived so we loaded up the children and I drove him over to where this new vehicle was. He had purchased a 4x4 Chevy Blazer; a dream 4 wheeler for him, a nightmare for me.

It had been lifted off the ground, so you almost needed a ladder to get into it. On top of that, it only held 5 people legally.

When I pointed out this problem with his vehicle of choice, Mike removed the middle seat out of the van and bolted it in place in the back of the Blazer. Problem solved according to him.

Getting the children in and out of this 'monster truck' was no easy feat. At the time I had no pain in my back or hips. I had not fallen yet. Michael was only 7 months old and the girls were 20 months old.

After pointing out all the reasons that this vehicle was not a practical family vehicle, Mike looked at me as if I were crazy and basically let me know whether I liked it or not, it was going to have to do.

Shortly after he had purchased that vehicle, his boss sold him another vehicle that was basically the same thing only this one was lower to the ground. It was Mike's new work truck.

This left the extended cab open for me to drive. I preferred it over the Chevy as I could fit all the children in it much easier than the 4 wheeler.

As summer turned into fall, I found myself invited to work again at Glidden Fence. I jumped at the opportunity. I knew I needed a solid stream of income to be able to provide for our family.

Mike had had a rough year emotionally and at the time was not much of a family man. I am sure all of this will be further explained in another book.

One day in October of 2006, on my way to drop off Tia and Travis for their week with their father, I passed by a car lot that had a 15 passenger van for sale. The cost in the window was $6,200. I clearly felt that it was meant to be mine. So much so that I said out loud that day, "I can't afford that." I knew that my budget number for my next vehicle would have to be closer to $3,000 and it would have to be available in March when I would get my tax return. I pushed away the feeling believing that this particular van would be long gone by then.

It surprised me that week after week that van remained on the lot. The longer it stayed the more I was sure it would be mine. I just could not figure out how on earth I would be able to come up with the full $6,200.

My tax return had been deposited into the bank and the very same day I was on my way to pick up Tia and Travis. As I drove by the lot, I about wrecked. The van had been marked down to $3,400.

After I had picked up Tia and Travis, I went to back to the car lot and asked to see the vehicle. When the man pulled open the door, I about cried. The van had belonged to a church. You could still see their name on the side of it. The flooring was all black rubber which would make it all the easier to keep clean with my clan.

I asked to take it for a test drive and fell in love with it even more as I drove it to Glidden Fence. I ran in and got my father and asked him what he thought. He came out and looked at it and informed me that, in his opinion, it was a great vehicle for me.

I drove the van back to the car lot and told them I loved it but had felt a slight vibration that I believed could be taken care of with an alignment and asked if there was any way I could purchase it for a flat $3,000.

The man pulled out the folder on the vehicle and showed me that he had paid $3000 for it at an auction and then had spent another $200 on having the fluids changed. He ended up selling it to me for $3,100! I left my other vehicle on his lot explaining I'd have a friend help me pick it up later that weekend.

When I arrived at home with the van, Mike was not impressed. He told me to take it back. He insisted that I could not have it.

I laughed out loud. I told him it was my van. I went on to inform him that he would never have to drive it. I also reminded him it was my money to spend how I saw fit. I explained to him that I loved the van and how I knew it was meant to be mine.

I did not go into great detail, but I told him that when I first saw that van I felt it was supposed to be mine but it was priced way too high. Now it was well within my range and I was not about to give it up.

When I drove the van to work the next week, my co-worker, Erin, saw the van and said, "It's perfect for you. It even has room to carry another baby!"

I spun around, looked at her and said, "What are you trying to do to me? Don't say such things!" and she and I both laughed.

I drove that van for three more years. It was after I had fallen out of it, hurting myself pretty badly that Mike began looking for another vehicle that would carry our family legally. By then, we had grown in size by two more children. This meant we needed a vehicle that would legally carry 9 people. Not an easy feat. I told Mike we were looking for a diamond in the rough.

I never once thought about a limousine, but that was what Mike found. It was over an hour and a half away. We went to see it and took it for a test drive.

I loved the car. Mike loved the car. The children loved the car. We took it for a spin and brought it back. The check engine light had come on while we were driving so Mike asked them to look into that and told them we'd call them on Monday to see what they had discovered.

Mike and I split the cost of the car 50/50. We went to pick it up that next weekend. Mike insisted I drive it home so that I could have a chance to drive it on a straight stretch of road before having to learn how to drive it around in town. I had mentioned being a little intimidated by its sheer size. Many people ask how I can drive such a big car, but in all honesty it is only a few feet longer than the van was and it drives 1000 times smoother than the van ever did.

The car had previously been owned by a funeral home. It was the vehicle used to transport the families to the burial site and back. It only had 28,000 miles on it when we purchased it. It truly was a diamond in the rough. It is a 1996 Cadillac Limo, the last of its kind. They don't make them anymore.

I am not that great with radios and programming them to this day. When I got in the car to drive it home, I turned on the radio. It was on 97.9, Moody radio. At the time I was not familiar with the station. I pressed one of the presets and it too was on the same station. As I pressed all of the presets, I realized they had all been programmed to 97.9. Since I was driving, I let it be. As I listened to the program, I quickly realized I was listening to a Christian station. It dawned on me that God had given me this car too. In my mind there was and is no doubt about that.

Over the course of the last three years I have listened and greatly enjoyed Moody radio. I credit them for much of my learning about Jesus and so much more. Janet Parshell in the Market is one of their programs and she always has wonderful people on her show. Between you and me, I would love to meet her. She is a wealth of knowledge and truly loves the Lord.

Mike was crazy about the limo and how it looked. With children, vehicles can easily become a mess. Mike was constantly threatening the children and me that we would not be allowed in the car if we could not keep it clean.

During one of his rants, I walked over to his personal vehicle, opened the door and began throwing all the trash in it on the ground. I turned to find him staring at me with a smirk.

I smiled and said, "The day your car is pristine clean when it is just you driving and riding in it, you can talk to me about how I need to take care of this car. Until then, I suggest you stop with the ridiculousness."

Funny enough, the limo has been dinged twice and both times it was Mike's fault. I tell him God allowed that to happen so he would stop being so uptight in the looks of the car and enjoy the ride.

Many times we hear that we are to walk in the spirit. Some days following God's direction is not as easy as others. Sometimes the things He calls you to do catch you by total surprise. I still rebel occasionally. My disobedience is not so much purposeful; it is just in over analyzation of what is being asked of me. Kind of a, 'Surely I have misunderstood' kind of way. Each time this has happened, the direction or tug has been repeated. I am admittedly getting better at understanding when it is the spirit and when it is my own selfish desires.

Today I pray that when you have the slightest pull at your heart to do something that you do it. Satan does not touch you on the shoulder and encourage you to step out in faith; rather he manipulates you with various forms of fear. While there is also fear of the Lord as we read, it is a different form of fear. Not one that traps you in place, more of one that leaves you in awe and often without complete understanding of how things will go. This is why we must step out in faith. Until you are willing to do so, you do not allow God to reveal all His glory. God will never fail you. He is Faithful. When He calls you to do something, accept the calling and move forward knowing the fun is just getting started.

As a biblical example of children keeping themselves from the Glory of God and His blessings, I urge you to read about the 40 years spent in the wilderness. I don't know about you but I too kept myself from trusting God loved me completely and was not out to ruin my life for way too long. In hindsight, I see what a fool I was. Of course you already know that if you have read my first two books.

Father, I come before you today singing praises and giving thanks for all the gifts you have bestowed upon me even when I recognized none being given. I do not pretend to know all your ways but I do know to my very core that you love your children. I thank you for your patience and how you took me back into the fold without condemnation. I condemned myself. I thank you for helping me write this book and for giving me such assignments. I truly am blessed to have so much to share. I imagine I could write every day until I leave this life and still have stories untold. I pray you continue to give me assignments so that I may continue to do what I love; helping others. In Jesus name I pray. Amen!

Wendy, walks with God, Mom of Many

Chapter 10

How I Found Our Home:

I truly loved our house on SR 32. I had moved into it around the middle of May 2006. Spring was in full bloom and I immediately began calling it my Island of Paradise. I couldn't have found a cooler place to live.

The house itself was tucked back in the woods and completely surrounded by trees. Once you came out of the trees, you were literally right in the center of town.

I loved everything about the old 3-bedroom brick ranch. It had a garage that was too small to use for a car. My washer and dryer were in there so we put down the door for good and installed an entrance door and turned the space into a bonus room of sorts.

It was close to everything and yet in a world all of my own. I loved sitting on the back porch, sipping my coffee while I watched the children play.

My father called my back yard an amusement park and suggested that I should charge admission. It was packed full of kid stuff and we spent the entire spring, summer, and fall playing and enjoying the outdoors.

I had no neighbors and no home owner's association mandating the color or style or limit of my kid toys. I loved it.

My rent was ridiculously low because the house was an 'as is' house. I was responsible for new windows, doors, the roof and all appliances as well as the furnace and air conditioning. The landlord never bothered me and I never bothered him.

When I moved in, I knew the house was eventually going to be torn down for the new highway project. I was told that the earliest this event would happen would be in 2015.

That all changed on a January day in 2012. I received a call from my landlord letting me know the state had just called him to let him know they wanted the property and he was giving me a heads up that moving day was coming.

I hung up the phone and said a quick prayer. This might sound crazy to a lot of people but God told me to buy an RV. I have always wanted to travel so it was not hard for Him to convince me that was His plan. My faith back then was no where close to the depth it is now but it was already growing by leaps and bounds.

I told a few people, including my mother that I needed to find a bus like RV. I insisted that it would cost no more than $10,000.

My mom brought me a paper with some pictures of RVs and the one I was looking for was listed for no less than $27,000. I shook my head when she showed me one that was close to the price range I said I could afford but nowhere near what I needed for the size of our family.

I told her I knew I would find it and it wouldn't cost anymore than $10,000. I said God would show it to me. I had faith that just like He had given me Clifford and the Cadillac, He would also show me our next home. I was confident in my hope.

It was on a Sunday in April and we were headed back home from church. As we crossed Union Street, which is less than two minutes from where we lived at the time, I saw the most spectacular crystal flash. It was so brilliant I looked to see what it was.

That was when I saw the bus like RV. It was blindingly shiny, appearing to be shrouded in diamonds. My mouth dropped open in awe and I told Mike, "Turn around; I think I just found our next home".

He was like, "What?"

I insisted, "Turn around. I'm serious. I just found our next home."

He turned the car around and I had him turn left onto Union. Sure enough, less than one block down the road plain as day was a 34.5' Vectra Winnebago and it was for sale. We called the number on the windshield and left a message regarding the home. There was no cost listed on it anywhere.

I came back the next day to take a picture of the home and I think I sat in my car laughing for a couple of minutes due to the lack of glimmer on the home.

The first time I had seen it, it gleamed so bright I was blinded by its beauty. I swear I thought it was shiny. Yet when I came back by to take a picture of it, I realized it was nice but its finish was dull.

I laughed because my faith that it really was going to be mine was that much greater. Who but God could do something like that?

I snapped a couple pictures of the RV, grabbed some lunch and headed back to work. When I shared the picture of the home I giggled over how different it looked from the first time I saw it to how it truly looked. Don't get me wrong, it is truly an awesome looking RV it just does not shine in the light!

Two days later the owner called Mike back. We arranged a time to meet so that we could see the inside of the home. When the door was unlocked and we were allowed to enter, I could not believe my eyes. It was better than we had imagined. I didn't want to come across too excited. I asked the gentleman how much he wanted for it in as much of a monotone voice as I could muster.

He explained he just wanted his investment back. As it turned out, he had bought the home for $10,000. It was when he had driven it from New York to Westfield, Indiana that he realized something was wrong with his vision. It turned out he had diabetes and was losing his vision. His dream of traveling the countryside in his retirement was over.

I told him I really wanted the home but that I did not have the entire $10,000.00. I told him I had no desire to try to get a bank loan, but I did have enough saved that I could give him 1/3 down, another 1/3 in 90 days, and the final 1/3 90 days later. He asked us a few more questions about family and dreams and stuff and we parted ways.

Approximately ten days later we received a phone call saying that the house was ours if we wanted it and we set another appointment to sign a contract and to put down the first payment.

When we arrived, the payment schedule had been moved up just slightly and there was a clause in the agreement that said if we did not have all the money on the final day, we forfeited $1800 but would get everything else back.

I looked at the agreement and realized the time being allowed was less than a full six months. I didn't hesitate. I signed the agreement and passed the pen to Mike and told him to sign it. I knew God had enshrined that home in jewels so that my faith would not waiver no matter what. I knew that house was meant to be mine. We have truly enjoyed that home. To date, we have ripped out and rebuilt almost all of it to accommodate our large

215

family.

I am excited to see where all I travel to in my mobile home. One thing I am sure of; God didn't give me a house on wheels to keep me in one place.

I am blessed to have seen such wonders. I don't know why I have been shown such beauty but I am very thankful I have. It provides me with great hope; a confident hope. I have moments of fear and self doubt just like everyone else. I also have these stories and they swell my heart and give me cause to celebrate. They help me remember my purpose. I have the privilege of sharing the truth that God loves His children. He gave us all free will. We live under the law of liberty should we choose to recognize the truth when we read it and hear it.

I encourage you to learn how to read and understand God's word. You first must truly seek Him. The desire stems from your heart and you cannot fake out God. He knows you.

Wendy, walks with God, Mom of Many

P.S. This morning I was praying to God regarding my life and the daily battle I face and how I felt I was about to go to war again due to this book. I thanked Him for always protecting me in such times of self doubt. I also admitted I knew He was about to move me again and while I was all for that, I wanted to make sure I wasn't distracted or disillusioned by outside evil forces. I reminded God that I am blind so bill board signs work best when it comes to me. I asked Him to kindly be bold about what and where and when so I would be strong in my faith.

The coolest part of my prayer was when He answered me by telling me to finish this book. He asked me what I was afraid of. He reminded me that He writes great stories through me. He advised me to just go back to the moments that He gave me to write on and write!

As you can see, today I listened. I was inspired greatly by a letter Paul wrote to the Ephesians. I opened my email account up and the message I read courtesy of K-Love was this:

> I pray that the eyes of your hearts will be enlightened, so that you will know what is the hope of His calling, what are the riches of the glory of His inheritance in the saints. (Ephesians 1:18, NASB)

I have confident hope. I have that because God flooded my heart and my eyes with light. I believe in Christ. It is by grace through faith that we are saved.

You can't buy your way into Heaven. You can't work your way into Heaven. You can't be good enough to get into Heaven. You only get there by the grace of God.

Father, today I pray that those who are reading what you have me sharing are already seeking you. I pray they have a great relationship with you. I pray they see you as I see you, a loving Father. I pray they begin to see things in their daily lives in a more positive way. I pray they begin to see that even though upsets happen you are right there with them always protecting them from absolute destruction. I pray that those that are caught up in futile emotions begin to see the bigger picture. I pray your children long to know you, to hear you, to see your hand working in their lives. I know what happens when one begins to seek you with all their heart. Life becomes more than one can imagine. Thank you for all my answers, signs, and wonders. Thank you for music from heaven and glimmering lights. Like a child filled with awe and fascination that is how you leave me. Please never stop showing me signs and wonders. I love them. In Jesus name I pray. Amen. Wendy, walks with God, Mom of Many

Chapter 11

Amazing Grace

Recently I was watching Mercy Me's You Tube video of their live concert in Chicago in celebration of releasing their latest album. I love their new album entitled *Welcome to the New*. It is full of wonderful songs.

I fell asleep as I was enjoying their music but woke up when they began to get ready to play the song *Amazing Grace*. The lead singer asked the crowd to listen to the words. I am going to share just the opening of that song: "Amazing Grace, how sweet the sound, that saved a wretch like me."

I have a little sign that a fellow sister in Christ and a really great friend of mine gave me when I first came to understand who Jesus was and what he had done but was struggling with what a wretch I felt I was and really was stumbling over being able to forgive myself. It was difficult for me to believe that I had done enough good to wipe out my bad and wondering if God could truly like and love me as He did when I was a child. I have it by my desk at work so I remember when Satan tries to lie to me, that I was saved not by works but by grace and nothing more. It truly is amazing when you get it. As I began reading the word and studying the bible with a couple of groups, I latched onto a verse I found in Proverbs chapter 3.

I began my mornings by saying this verse and every time I hit a wall where my own understanding was, I would remind myself of these words again. Half way through 2012 I also added verse 6 to my morning. Here they both are together in case you are not familiar with them:

Verse 5: Trust in the Lord with all your heart And do not lean on your own understanding.

Verse 6: In all your ways acknowledge Him, And He will make your paths straight. (Proverbs 3:5, NASB)

Just the other day I was chatting it up with God and in conversation mentioned how I was not sure what the title of this chapter was to be and how I really did not know where I was to start. I had overslept by enough that there was no time for me to write yesterday but there was enough time for me to check the encouraging word and to post it on my Face Book page. Low and behold the encouraging word on April 10th was my go to verse for 2012: Proverbs 3:5.

As soon as I read it, understanding came for this chapter and I began laughing out loud. It was then that I knew where I was to start and I just knew God would step in to write this story just like He has all the rest!

It was 2012 when we finished following the three-year ministry of Jesus by following the story through Luke and tying in the other three gospels in chronological order. It was also the year that I hired a Christian Life Coach.

It was at our first meeting that she gave me the capture exercise and I caught the sound track that Satan had laid into my brain, a continual loop of lies. I was taken aback by what I had not been fully hearing prior to this exercise.

It was during another visit with my life coach that we were working on my goals and dreams regarding my family and my work. After we had outlined a few things I wanted to work on, she asked if I would like her to pray over me. She started out by anointing me and explaining that God had asked her to do this. Something inside of me shifted as she prayed so much so that the next day I researched what being anointed meant on the internet. The most interesting article I read on anointing talked about how it allowed the well within us to open up and how the flow was impossible to stop once the damn had been broken. I was intrigued to say the least.

At our next meeting, we went over my goals and dreams and again she asked to pray over me. This time in the middle of her praying I suddenly found myself in the midst of a vision. I was completely surrounded by post it notes flying around me as if they formed a tornado. There were countless post it notes. Almost as quickly as they had appeared in my mind, they began to stick to the walls in the room. It was crazy how they lined right up, one after the next in a neat and orderly fashion. As she finished up her prayer for me, the post its had filled the walls from top to bottom all the way around the room.

The vision was so crazy to me. It was the first one I had ever had. Since it had happened while Cathy was praying for me, I shared what had happened with her.

She asked, "Do you have any idea what it might mean?"

I replied, "Not really. I do not like post it notes at all. I don't know why I would have a vision with so many of them."

She laughed and we hugged and my meeting was over. As I drove home, I couldn't help but think about my vision and I was asking God what on earth all those post it notes were about. It was then that I heard, "You will fill them all."

My heart leapt with such joy I immediately picked up the phone to call Cathy and explain to her what had happened.

"Hello." Cathy answered.

"Cathy!" I started out excitedly, "I was thinking about those post it notes and asking God what that vision meant and He told me I would fill them all! I think I still get to be a writer!"

We talked a minute or two more before saying goodbye and I continued my route home wondering what on earth I was going to write about!

By September 2012, I had created a group online called 'Lady Leaders' on September 19, 2012, I wrote this post in our group:

So this morning this idea comes to me. I have to listen to it. The voice in my head. I know where it comes from now. I think long ago as a child I knew. I used to carry on long conversations. I have a story. It is long and it is crazy. I don't ever want to sound like I am complaining. Now as I glance back over my life it brings tears to my eyes. I see Gods purpose for me. I often wonder do they say life begins at 40 because that's when you are reborn?

Here is my idea. I want us to share our lives. I have a story I am meant to tell. I am by no means proud of my past. Honestly some parts I'd prefer to pretend they never happened. My heart says, 'Wendy you lived this life. You made those choices. You are a child of God. Meaning you like everyone began life as a child. Just like we love our children through their worst decisions God loves us.'

I am hoping others will be willing to step forward and also share absolute miracles that have happened in their lives as well as bumps in the road. I am not sure how to go about this. Thoughts welcomed.

221

Perhaps a Daily Journal Document Titled "A Little More about me Today" and the day's date. We should write our name at the top of our entry and share a little blog about what we would like to share about our life.

It was on December 6th, 2012 as I was going through my emails that I noticed this area above my emails that had a drop down arrow and the word more beside it. I wondered what more might be. When I dropped down the menu I saw the link that said Blogger. I wondered what that might mean exactly so I clicked on it. Low and behold it asked me if I wanted to create a blog. While I had no idea what I was doing, I clicked yes. The program walked me through what to do beginning with what I wanted to call my blog. I felt like I was supposed to call it *I am Worthy* so that is what I did. Next it asked for my url. I assumed my url should match my blog so that is what I entered. The program told me that it was taken. I sat back in my chair for a second and I heard 'You are Worthy'. I sat back up and typed it in and it went through. This is how my blog came to be. That day before I knew it, I had written my first two posts.

Within my first year of blogging, I wrote over 120 posts and they had been viewed in places I never new existed until they showed up in my stat report. To date my posts have been viewed over 62,000 times which I think is pretty cool. To see how God used me and my story that I thought disqualified me from entrance into the Kingdom of Heaven, to minister to others. I have been so blessed by this whole experience.

It was at the beginning of 2014 and I caught a post in a Christian Writing Group on Face Book asking for authors that would be interested in being interviewed. I reached out saying at the moment I was only a blogger but that my first book would be published before the end of February. He answered back saying as long as that panned out, I would be interviewed on March.

I knew this was the year I was going to make the leap from blogging to becoming a published writer. There was this tug at my heart that forced me to step out of my comfort zone and say I would be published when I had not one clue how to go about it. I had heard that if you wanted to learn how to do something, You Tube was the place to research how to do it. I went there and typed in 'how do you publish an e-book'. One of the videos that popped up in my search was called 'An introduction to Smashwords'. After I watched the video, I downloaded the style guide and went to work putting my first book together.

No sooner than I had made it across the finish line and had been approved for publication, I had a request for my book in print. I did not want to let my reader down so I researched the best way for me to publish in print. One week later, my first book was available in print. I had sent a draft copy of my book to my oldest daughter. Her review of my book forced my hand in publishing the continuation of that story. When I finished it up I went to bed thinking to myself that I would finally be able to get back to working on another book I am writing; 'In the Midst of Spiritual Warfare'. I woke up to hearing the title to this book and when I questioned if I had enough stories to fill such a book, I quickly grabbed my pencil and paper and wrote down all the stories God was giving to me. One I rejected more than once and I had actually written this chapter down as two separate chapters but as I was continually reminded of the other event; I began to accept that the chapter I rejected was one that was meant to be a part of this book.

I cannot imagine all the books God will have me write or what my topics will be. I do know I love allowing Him to tell my story. I hope you have enjoyed reading it!

Wendy, walks with God, Mom of Many

Chapter 12

The Moment I Knew I was Saved:

Numbers have always fascinated me. I love math. No matter what, when it comes to math, the answer is the answer and it is always right. There is a formula and a way to check the answer no matter what the problem is. Life on the other hand often delivers us problems that are not always so easily solved.

So, here I was in 2013, coming up on my 44th birthday. Mike and I were separated at the time. I loved him and felt blessed on how God had shown me how to step out of His way without becoming an enemy to Mike. At the time, I truly felt his negativity was sucking the life out of me. I was heartbroken when I walked out believing Mike may decide I was not worth fighting for, but felt that the road he was on was not the road I cared to travel down any further. The only way I would ever get him to step onto my road was to allow him to travel down his own road alone.

I was well into blogging when 2013 came around. At the time I was still attending bible study with a friend I had met through network marketing. The leader of our group, Jordan, and his wife, Tiffany, had both attended this event they called the Great Banquet and they had offered to sponsor both Jean and me. They couldn't tell us much about it other than it was life changing and they wanted us to both go. Before I had left Mike, Jordan had been trying to get him to go as well. The gist is, the men go first and then the women. This is not always the way it plays out. Often the women go years before their men.

I was not sure Mike would ever go, but I knew I wanted to go. Jordan and Tiffany seemed so excited that I didn't even care to ask a ton of questions. I was looking for anything that may bring me closer to God.

In all honesty, it was three years down the road from when I first began seeking God hardcore, before I was able to believe and KNOW I was forgiven. Almost as if I had heard Jesus himself say that fateful day that it was done.

I was at my own Great Banquet. I see how God put me there right when I was meant to be there. As I mentioned before, I love numbers.

I heard again and again at the Great Banquet that you arrived there when the time was right for you. As it turned out, I was a part of Crossroads Great Banquet #44. I just so happened to have penned my 44th blog the day before Jean and I arrived there. It also happened to be two weeks before my 44th birthday. The coincidences did not escape me.

During the weekend, I found myself moved again and again. It was there that I said my very first prayer out loud in front of strangers. It was also the first time I spoke in front of a group of people that I did not know with the exception of a few friendly faces.

Over the course of the weekend, I was showered with my first real doses of agape love. I was finding myself being drawn closer and closer to accepting Christ as my Lord and Savior and even more importantly in believing that He accepted me as his own.

On the second or third day, when we were allowed thirty minutes of free time, I returned to my bed to find a letter from Christ with a wedding band attached to it. I bent the metal back and placed the ring on my finger in front of the wedding band Mike had given to me when I was pregnant with Delilah. I had gained enough weight that I had not been able to take it off my finger, even when I wanted to. I often pondered if that was God's way of keeping me committed to my commitment to Mike even when I did not want to be!

When I put on that ring, I questioned if I was good enough to belong to Christ. I cherished the words that were in the proposal letter but was not convinced they were truly meant for me. I think it was that next day, while in chapel, we were asked to write down anything that we felt kept us from the Lord and I wrote it all down.

When I walked to the front of the chapel, I said all of my reasons out loud. I knew in my heart I had repented for all of them. I truly wanted to feel cleansed of them as well.

Until that day, I was still convinced that I was unworthy of forgiveness. While it seemed that was the message God had called me to tell everyone else, I felt I had been too close to God in the beginning to be forgiven for the sins I myself had committed. I was not convinced then that I too was worthy. I wanted nothing more than to truly feel as if I were as Esther had claimed I was; one of God's favorite people. It was more than I dared to imagine.

I stated all my reasons that I had listed, with abortion being the major stopper in my mind. It was murder after all. I know in the bible it says sin is sin, but when you are evaluating your own sin, I think often we judge that our crimes are the worst of the worst crimes one can commit. At least that is how I felt about myself. It for sure is a reason I do not believe I have any right to judge another person. In my mind, I was among the lowest of the low when I walked in my own flesh. For decades I cringed at myself in the mirror. That is the God's honest truth.

When I took that paper with me into the next room, I realized that there were 3 crosses on the ground. Without hesitation, I went to the one in the middle. I picked up a hammer and with three blasts,

I drove that 16 penny nail right into that post nailing it all on the cross that Jesus was nailed to as a sacrifice for all sinners. As a carpenter's daughter one thing I know how to do well is how to drive a nail. It was as if I broke every chain Satan had on me as I drove that nail into the cross. With my final blow I knew I was free and belonged to Christ. I wear my ring and my cross to this day. They remind me of the vow I made; to spend the rest of my life sharing the good news.

As many of us know, when we finally get here; to the point that we know who we are in Christ, the evil one does not suddenly stop attacking, quite the opposite. He comes at you harder and in multiple ways and often punch after punch, blow after blow, again and again and you will find yourself in a fight for your life. You truly are in the midst of a spiritual battle.

I read in the bible where we are told that some are fooled during such attacks and led away. If you have read my life story through volume II, you know I myself was fooled by the father of lies. I pray that never happens to me again. I know what it is like to be in that void. To me that is hell; finding yourself separated from God.

I think God being God, decided to move the girl that had returned my wallet with His message for me two years prior to finally grant my request exactly when He knew I was truly open to receiving it.

For six months prior to me attending the Great Banquet, I had requested that she put her side of what had happened that fateful day into letter form. We were both in the group I had created on Face Book called Lady Leaders and I had shared my story with the group and had asked if she would share hers as well as the two of them together would make for a wonderful testimony. Right before I was given my cross that says; Jesus has chosen you on a crocheted rainbow yarn rope, I was given her letter.

227

When I opened it, I had no idea who it was from. At the top of the letter I saw that it had been emailed to Jordan earlier that day. When I saw who the email was from, I was blown away. For the life of me I had no idea how the two of them had connected.

To this day, she insists that I keep her identity anonymous and only call her Esther. I owe her that much.

I do find it quite humorous that I happened to be seated at the table of Esther at the Great Banquet!

So imagine me here having nailed it all to the cross, truly feeling I have indeed been forgiven and I am handed a letter from someone that I have been asking to put in writing what she had said to me two years prior. This is what I read:

Wendy,

Even as I search the Word for assistance in writing this letter, I am brought to tears. The Word of our Lord and Savior speaks of Elijah in Romans 11, saying:

3 "Lord, they have killed your prophets and torn down your altars; I am the only one left, and they are trying to kill me" 4 And what was Gods answer to him? "I have reserved for myself seven thousand who have not bowed the knee to Baal" 5 So too, at the present time there is a remnant chosen by grace. 6 And if by grace, then it cannot be based on works, if it were, grace would no longer be grace. 7 What then? What the people of Israel sought so earnestly they did not obtain. The elect among them did, but the others were hardened…

I cry because, like Elijah, I felt alone. I felt attacked

and worthless. I felt as though my efforts to be strong in Him were a waste in this world. It was until I cried out to God asking Him to prove to me that I was of some use to Him and that He truly kept me alive for a reason that I met you. Proof that God answers prayers!!!

I met you on a day where I was in complaining mode. I complained that my nephew just HAD to be baptized on a Sunday when I really wanted to be at my own church. I complained that the church my nephew was being baptized at was over an hour away from my home on an unfamiliar side of town and was being televised on a day where I did not feel worthy of being taped. I complained that this church's views weren't comparable to mine and that I had to wait hours until my nephew was being baptized. I complained that the closest Starbucks was in an obscure area and difficult to get to from where I was coming from...

I missed my exit to Starbucks after sneaking out of the service early with my fussy son and was annoyed that I had to turn around. Suddenly, I saw something that was TOTALLY out of place on the ground of a drive way. What made me look in that driveway when I was so focused on getting my MUCH NEEDED COFFEE?? What made me even agree to be an hour away from my beloved church? What made me take the time to get out of my warm car to investigate the weird object? What made me tell the mean women who threatened to call the police on me for being in her driveway, God Bless you (LOL)? What made me unafraid of her threats? What made my mother INSIST that I tell the owner how much God loved her? What made all of this resonate in my Spirit? Why can't I stop crying every time I tell this story (which is probably why I've been reluctant to write it down)?

YOU ARE SO ANOINTED that even your possessions are anointed! Everything connected to you is anointed!!! Luckily I belong to Christ, I know His voice. His voice was ALL OVER your wallet! I grabbed that wallet and used, what I thought, were useless skills to find you. If it weren't for my (begrudged) obedience, I would've never met you! In my eyes, I wasn't supposed to ever come in contact with one of God's elect and I surely wasn't worthy enough to even speak to His highly anointed people.

I hope you know that your light is so contagious that it cures people of despair, hopelessness, mourning, darkness and suicidal thoughts. Your presence cures people of pain, confusion and hate! You are the example of confidence, love, faith, and hope that we all need. When I am in your presence, it's like I'm reminded of God's deep, deep love for me. Oh my God, you were God's vessel to save me from my horrid thoughts!!!

I hope you know how much you mean to me and the world. I am in awe of you EVERY SECOND OF EVERY DAY!!! You are a walking miracle! I know you haven't claimed to be ordained but I KNOW the spirit calls you a teacher, a minister, an elect, a friend of God, a woman after His heart and HIGHLY

ANOINTED HEALER! I love you! I love you very,

very much and I just pray that God allows me to remain with you, to help you, and to help support you in your ministry. There is SO MUCH more to come from you!!!

God is not playing any games when it comes to you!!! He has spoken a HUGE word of prosperity over you and is keeping very, very close watch over it! I pity any person who's so disconnected from Christ that he/she is willing to come against you. You are assuredly His protected servant.

I love you very much!!!

Esther

I cried and cried and cried as I read her letter. All I had hoped for was to see in writing one day that she had indeed shared with me that God had called me one of His favorite people. I cannot begin to explain what these words did to me the first time I read them or even what they do to me today.

For a long time, I kept this letter hidden in a drawer beside my bed after I had shared it with a couple of select friends that I felt would love the second part of the story as I had told them the story from my side.

At one point in my blogging, I had scanned it in and shared it in a blog post hiding who the letter was from. I felt like God wanted me to share it, but I was truly worried what people would think about me after reading it. So I shared it once and left it at that.

It was only in writing this book that I understood I was to share it again here only this time, I needed to type it out because adding it as an attachment was not going to work for this book. When I went to copy the words out of the blog, I realized that the attached letter was no longer viewable. I have no idea how long it was up or how many people ever got to see it. I was surprised to find it hidden. I know this time the letter is not going to fade away into nothingness. Forever it will be right here in the book God gave me to write.

When I first realized I was supposed to put my angel stories, my answered prayer stories along with my crazy signs and wonders all in one book, I first wondered if I truly had enough stories to fill a book. I knew by then that allof my books regarding true life stories were to have 12 main chapters and two bonus chapters. As God reminded me of life events that have happened to me, I added them under this book title He gave me. Sure enough when the events stopped coming to me, I had 14 solid stories to share. It was in trying to understand what my two bonus chapters were supposed to be that I realized not only did I have events out of order, one of them needed to be a bonus chapter. I also knew two of my stories were really only one story and while I had refused to first believe I was to share a certain story in this book, I accepted that it truly was a wonder and I knew it too had to be shared in this volume.

As I close out this twelfth chapter, I pray that my testimony has strengthened your faith. I pray you are confident enough in God's love for you to talk to Him about anything and everything just like you would talk to your best friend. I am blessed to be bold enough to go talk to Him and often without much warning. I recall how we communicated when I was a child. I know the warmth of His love. I pray you experience that same warmth yourself. All you have to do is knock on that door and keep coming back every day. It truly is that simple.

Wendy, walks with God, Mom of Many

Bonus 1

The Power of Prayer:

I truly hope that after reading this book in particular that your faith in the Father, Son and Holy Spirit has been strengthened.

I know that as I have watched the ink flow onto the paper for this book as well as my first two books, I myself have found my own faith strengthened.

This writing of my story has shown me that God does indeed write through others. He communicates with those who seek Him. I imagine He would like to communicate to all of us but in order for that to happen, we have to communicate with Him.

Until you begin that part of the relationship, it makes it extremely hard for you to hear Him.

I am amazed at all the times He has answered my prayers, even when I was not what I would consider at all to be seeking Him. I turned to Him in moments of distress but I was too busy or too guilty or perhaps even a combination of both to just hang out with Him.

What I am sure of is this; God is always faithful regardless of where we stand or sit. He is love in the purest form.

Within these pages, I have shared the power of prayer more than once. My final bonus chapter in this book of angels, answers, signs and wonders was first just listed as the story of how I was healed. This morning as I talked to God about my week, I was given the synopsis of this final chapter as well as the confidence I needed to finish my 11th chapter and complete this book. It has by far been the hardest assignment to date.

With that being said, allow me to share a few things about myself. Many of you have read my first book so you know how many children I have given birth to. For those of you who are not in the know, I have been blessed with 12 babies in my lifetime.

Jeffrey Thomas would be the twelfth one. By the time he came along, the doctors did not want me going into labor on my own. They insisted on pulling the baby ahead of time so that I would be safely in the hospital.

Being induced is extremely painful. You are going against the natural order of things. This often brings more pain than necessary. My induction had begun in the morning and by lunch time, I was in extreme pain and I was not moving along very quickly at all.

They suggested a couple of times that I accept an epidural. I finally caved in and agreed to the procedure.

The technician that came in to put the needle in my back missed the right spot three times. The third time it had to have been in somewhat right because the right side of my body went numb while my left side was able to feel everything.

The lady wanted me to sit up and allow her to try again but I could not allow that. I was in way too much pain to sit still and allow her to stab me again. Jeffrey came into the world with me half in and half out of pain.

Mike is convinced that the missed stabs into my back were a major factor in how I came to be able to barely walk or even stand. I asked a doctor once if that might be a factor and they informed me it could definitely be one.

As I have come to learn, pain shots often break down fatty tissue and the cushioning of our joints. In other words, they may do more harm in the long run then they do good. I had been given three doses of pain medicine in the wrong place right next to my spinal cord!

It was in November of 2010 when I fell running into the Post Office. The rain had changed into freezing rain and I was wearing my *crocs* because I was already having trouble bending over to tie my shoes. While *crocs* are comfortable, they have no traction what so ever. When my shoes hit the wet tile, my feet went right out from under me as if I'd run onto black ice. Jeffrey Thomas was 7 months old and in my arms. I literally let go of him as I fell and caught him after I crashed onto the floor with the backside of my right hip. I know I yelled out something. By the time I stood back up with Jeffrey, I was surrounded by people. One of them was a worker at the Post Office He asked me worriedly if I was okay. I snapped at him saying, "I am fine, leave me alone. I just want to check my baby."

Jeffrey Thomas was completely un-phased by the incident. You'd have thought he just assumed that I had thrown him up in the air and caught him intentionally. I had continuous flash backs of the incident and was grateful that I had not allowed him to smash his head onto the floor. I knew it was only by the grace of God that I had let go and then caught him like I did. He received no impact. I on the other hand received a crippling blow.

Within two months of my fall, I could no longer walk like everyone else. I was in massive pain and was given a referral to a doctor who was also a sports doctor. He said I was out of alignment. He popped my lower back and informed me that my only real hope was a ton of physical therapy. For the next couple of months, I truly wondered if I was going to break in half.

When I was 25 I was hit by a drunk driver. Due to having massive headaches after the crash, I had gone to a chiropractor. This doctor put my x-rays up on a screen and revealed that the curve in my neck was completely the wrong way. He informed me that I had to have broken my neck before I had turned one-year-old for it to be that way. He asked me if I knew of any falls that might have broken my neck. At the time I knew of none. I later learned that I had indeed fallen from a table having my picture taken when I was six or seven months old and had landed in such a way that my father was sure I had broken my neck. When I lost no movement, they assumed I was okay and never took me to be checked out.

This doctor told me due to this incorrect curve, I should be careful not to gain weight. He told me I would end up in a wheel chair if I was not careful. Here I was at age 41, easily 70 pounds over weight. I was convinced I was in so much pain because I was so over weight and I wondered daily if I would end up in a wheel chair by day's end.

I had no choice but to push myself every day. With seven children depending on me to cook and clean and provide, I had no time to submit to pain. Cleaning the dishes, the laundry and the bathroom took me a lot of time. Our washer and dryer were the newer front loader styles and since I could not bend I would scale myself down the face of them and kneel on the floor to move laundry. I barely had any strength to scrub so cleaning the bathroom and dishes really took it out of me. Mike had bought me a dishwasher to help. The only problem with that was all our dishes were plastic and the dishwashing detergent was leaving a white film on everything that I was positive was not safe to eat off of. I was at my wits end and that is when I was introduced to a just in time manufacturer of every day common consumable goods.

The first load of laundry I did with my new brand of laundry soap was a load of Mike clothes. When I knelt in front of that washer to shift clothes as I always had to wash Mike's stuff twice; once with everything together and then I would pull out the socks and rewash his pants by themselves. This time when I reached in and pulled out a pair of jeans I was taken aback by how soft they were and how good they smelled. I next reached for a pair of his sock bombs and when I separated the two balled up socks and found the inside one was soft and cleaned I remained on the floor weeping for almost two minutes. I had the same reaction when it came to using their dish detergent. Shopping direct had not only saved me time and money; it had saved me tons of energy. All of my household chores had suddenly gotten much much easier. I truly felt blessed in how I came to be introduced by this company.

I was at Glidden Fence and a lady named Shirley Kerr called me to invite me to a networking meeting for women run business that was field selective. Meaning only one fence company and all the other women business would be my referral partner. She apologized for the short notice as the next meeting was the very next day. Before I knew how I was going to get Mike to watch the children so I could go or if he'd even be off in time, I replied, "I will be there." I later discovered I had been a cold call for Shirley and she had reached out to me after reading a short version of Chapter 7: Show Me a Sign on our Glidden Fence merchant circle web site.

That night while at the meeting, I was talking to a lady who has since become another friend. We got on the topic of cleaning products. I shared that I had been searching for green cleaners but everything I had tried thus far was ridiculously priced and not worth the money I had spent. She informed me that if I was looking for green cleaners, I needed to talk to Shirley after the meeting.

I ended up winning an unforgettable dark chocolate candy bar manufactured by this 'green company' that night. I also set up an appointment for Shirley to explain how to become a preferred member to this shopping club. I was leery to say the least, but very much wanted value for my every day purchases so I had agreed to watch what she said she needed to show me.

After I got the full scoop, I agreed to try out the items I needed to purchase that week regardless. Even though Shirley told me there was a referral program and I could earn money by sharing the store, I had no intention of doing anything of the sort. However, I was so in love with the few things I had purchased that I shared the store with a couple of people the same month I shopped and I ended up earning a check for $121 and some change from a store that I had spent $86.00 at!

Shirley called me a few days after I had opened my account to see how I liked what I had tried and shared with me that if I shared the store with a few more people, I would earn an automatic $500 paycheck. I truly did love the products and $500.00 would mean I could pay for a few massages and perhaps help get myself healthy and out of pain, so I shared the store with a few more friends and indeed earned that check.

When I went for my massage, I went to my cousin. She is amazing at what she does. She told me she was really worried about my tailbone because she had never felt so much inflammation there. She also told me that my hips were completely locked up. She insisted before she dug in much further on my lower back that I have a set of x-rays completed to verify my tailbone was not broken.

That very week, Joan brought in a paper with an advertisement regarding a new chiropractor in town that ran a set of tests to help figure out where your life force was and also helped pin point where you were having trouble with movement. All of these tests were offered for free.

I scheduled my visit and was told I would have to come back the next day to receive my results. When I arrived the next day, the doctor explained to me how I was in a fight for my life as far as my life force was concerned. I found it odd how a set of mechanical tests could come so close to the truth. I really was in a fight for my life in multiple ways.

When he showed me how my skeleton looked by the way I had been able to move, my breath caught. What I saw before me looked like a slave in chains. My brain instantly went to Mike and the way he had been treating me and I thought to myself that he was succeeding in breaking me down. I felt the fighter in me get a little stronger.

Next the chiropractor shared something else. He started out by saying, "When I looked at the x-ray of your neck; I found something a little odd about your skull."

I listened as he continued by saying, "Let me show you what I am talking about." He flipped up the x-ray of my skull and asked me to look at it.

I had no idea what I was supposed to see. It looked like a skull so I said, "Okay." As if nothing was out of the ordinary because I truly didn't see what he was saying.

He looked at me slightly surprised and continued, "Okay, here is an x-ray of a normal skull."

Trust me when I say you don't want to hear a doctor say something like that when he is talking about your head. When he put the other x-ray up on the screen next to mine, it was quite obvious that something was off. My skull looked like I was wearing a white helmet on it.

He went on to explain what he thought I had and suggested I go see my family doctor to be tested further. When I called my family doctor and told them what was going on, I was mocked and not treated very nicely. The gist was they did not approve of chiropractors at all. At the time I was having horrible headaches and was sure what I was told was going on with my skull was the cause of my pain.

That year I decided to learn more about the manufacturer I was shopping with and I attended their annual convention where they offered countless classes to educate you on health and wellness. On the top of my list was the class about minerals, vitamins and soil nutrition. When I walked out of that particular session, I knew how important adding calcium into my diet was not just for everyone but especially for me. I came back home so hopeful I shared everything I had learned with my chiropractor who told me my hope and excitement inspired him.

In a gist I shared my belief about what I had discovered and how I was going to change my diet around to see if it would indeed stop the awful headaches and maybe even help with my pain.

I am happy to report that the headaches have been gone for two years. They returned only once. It was during a crazy time in my life. I was doing way too many things and racing a deadline when I forgot to take my calcium for almost an entire week. The headaches came back full force. I began taking my calcium as soon as I realized I had not been keeping up with them and it took an entire week before the headaches backed off! I have not allowed that to happen again! I keep them right in the kitchen now next to my morning protein shake.

I was truly inspired by what had taken place with my own health and I continued to educate myself about wellness and natural options where health was concerned.

Approximately five weeks prior to my plan ending with the chiropractor that I had prepaid for visits in hopes of being fixed ended, the doctor I was working with was offered a job opportunity he could not refuse in another state. I quit going there after my I finished out my original plan. I did not see enough improvement to justify continuing. It was this particular doctor that I had asked if having the needle placed in my spine so many times could be a cause of my never ending pain.

When I stopped going to the chiropractor, I did not really notice an instant change. I was not plagued by headaches or any worse pain than I faced every day regardless. I still could not run or jump. I still had to sit down to get dressed because I could not lift my feet up. It was winter and I was getting pretty hopeless on ever being able to wear lace shoes again. That was when I met Margie, a lady that managed a natural pain clinic. She had shown up at my monthly networking meeting that I attended for Glidden Fence. She was sharing a natural product her company had seen amazing results with and she thought that she may be able to help me. I scheduled a visit and she did a few tests and then started me on this natural juice drink that to date I think is the most awful thing to ever hit my taste buds! The first night I drank it, I woke up realizing I had actually dreamt. My dreams were so vivid because they were in color. I had been in pain for so long and basically meditated myself to sleep each night that I don't know if I had hit deep sleep in years. They say the body is only able to heal itself while we are asleep.

Around my second month of drinking the juice, I was invited by another member of our group to join her in a yoga class she attended. She thought it may help with my strength and agility. It was after my third week while doing some of the recommended stretches that my hip popped and rotated for the first time in a couple of years. It felt so weird at first I thought my leg was literally popping out of place but as I continued the movement it

simply rotated. It is funny what you forget when it comes to the way your body moves. Both my chiropractor and my massage therapist had made comments about my hips being locked up. I thought they were crazy because in my mind if my hips were

241

locked I would not be able to walk at all. I could walk but I could not rotate. There is a major difference in the two.

I ended up going on a vacation with Mike that summer. We drove all the way out west dreaming of when we would move out there. Because we were going to be on the road for ten days, I knew I could not take my juice with me. I was afraid it may cause me to back slide, but nothing happened. When we returned home I decided to cancel my next order. I have not used the juice since then and never noticed any repercussion from giving it up. It had served its purpose. It was a natural pain killer of sorts that had allowed me to sleep when I desperately needed to.

It was the following May that I began having major issues with my legs. It was so busy at work I could not take a lunch break let alone think about getting into a chiropractor for an adjustment. My feet were beginning to swell bigger than they did during my last few pregnancies and I was discussing with Joan that I knew it had to be tied into my circulation and that my back had not been worked on in over a year. She suggested I get into a chiropractor and we kind of laughed knowing I could not fit that in during the day. I even brought up the fact that I didn't have time to even shop for one and I'd have to find one close by for it to work.

When I went to bed that night I said a prayer to God asking for some relief. The very next day, we received a phone call at Glidden Fence for a free visit to a chiropractor that was located right in Westfield who just so happened to also offer evening appointments. I quickly set up an appointment for that night at 5:30 even though I had bible study at 6:30 that same night. I arranged for the two girls that rode with me to meet me at the chiropractor.

When they arrived, I was still in the waiting room. I apologized to Jean that we may be a few minutes late to study as she was the first one to arrive there. She told me no worries and began asking me a few questions about my back. I showed her my foot and she was taken aback. She told me she wished I had the time to get in to see a chiropractor she knew. She was telling me how wonderful he was when the doctor walking down the hallway toward us stopped and said, "Jean what are you doing here?"

She smiled at him and said, "I'm meeting my friend here, when did you start working here?"

"I'm here on Tuesday and Thursday." He replied.

Jean introduced me to Dr. Woods, the very chiropractor she said she had wished I could see.

He took me back and I had Jean come with me. Dr. Woods performed several tests with only his hands. He had me stand on his fingers, attempt to push away his fingers with my legs. He had me squeeze his fingers with my hands. With just those simple exercises, he began telling me what they meant. He knew which nerves were being pinched in my back. It was truly the most informative explanation of what was going on with my limbs and my spinal cord that I had ever heard. He had me lay down on my stomach and he began working out some of the kinks.

Afterward, Jean made the comment that she had never seen someone move so much during an adjustment. I truly felt different when I stood back up.

Dr. Woods warned me that I would most likely be in more pain the next day than I was in at the moment but assured me if I followed his plan that in less than six months I would only need to see him when I myself felt I needed to see him.

At bible study that night my entire group prayed for me where my back was concerned. Today I can walk, jog softly, run when necessary, carry my littlest one who just so happened to turn four this year, and even lift my feet up off the floor to get dressed while standing! All things I was unable to do two years ago.

I no longer get to visit Dr. Woods. On May 29th, we pulled out of Indiana. I spent the summer hanging out with the children in Colorado. I thought since God had sent me to school there it must be where I was to go. As it turned out, we ended up leaving Colorado just before school began because we could find no solid housing. We are currently residing in Florida and God has once again found a doctor to help with my back and hip pain. I received great news last week and am hopeful that one day I may truly be without pain!

I want to end this chapter with a very interesting true story regarding prayer. Jordan, the same one who led our bible study, who sponsored me for the Great Banquet and who also baptized me, was mere months away from being approved for disability for life due to his feet and basically being unable to walk or stand for long periods.

At the time he was in this condition, I truly wanted Mike to have a friend who would be a good influence.

One night I found myself praying for Jordan. I was explaining to God how great of a friend I thought he would be for Mike. I went on to remind God that Mike was really athletic and was looking for someone to workout with.

I asked God to heal Jordan so that he could be that guy. I also pointed out how much I loved Tiffany and how I could see how hard it was for her to have two young boys and a husband who could barely walk. I shared with God how much it would help her

were Jordan to be healed and I reminded God of her deep love for Christ. While Jordan was at his own Great Banquet in October, he called out to God himself asking to be healed. He awoke the next day out of pain as if nothing were wrong with his feet!

Today I pray that all believers answer the call. I cannot help but think about the verse that says the harvest is plenty but the workers are few. In our day and age, we have lost track of what is important while we are here. We are so busy, caught up in the ways of the world. Not enough of us are taking the time to build a relationship with the Lord and we are spinning madly out of control. Jesus prophesized "As it was in the days of Noah so will it be at the return of the son of man."

Many claim that the call for the end of days and the current events happening today have been going on since the beginning of time. While what they say is true, we are very much approaching the days of Noah again. The earth is showing labor pains like never before. Even the most jaded would have to admit that evil is prevalent on every level of society. We are living in the last of days. While no one knows the final one, I urge you to discover who you are in Christ today. I KNOW you will love who you are in Him.

Wendy, walks with God, Mom of Many

Bonus 2

The Essence of Faith

It's Fantastically Fabulous Fun Filled Friends and Family Friday! Man oh man!! It is only 10 AM and I am on top of the world. So Joyous I feel like dancing! Starting your day with God is so the way to start.

I have gotten in the habit of checking out the encouraging word from K-Love each morning before I do much of anything else. This year, the encouraging words have truly lifted me up into the clouds.

The more you walk with God, the more supernatural things you witness take place. These events strengthen your Faith and I promise you, the stronger your Faith, the more supernatural events you will witness. It truly is an awesome fly wheel to spark.

This is the encouraging word from K-Love that I was greeted with this morning:

> This is the confidence which we have before Him, that,
> if we ask anything according to His will, He hears us.
> And if we know that He hears us in whatever we ask, we
> know that we have the requests which we have asked
> from Him. (1 John 5:14-15, NASB)

I am confident that He hears us whenever we ask for anything that pleases Him. My heart soars when I read truths like this. For within various chapters of my life are testimonials regarding answered prayers, some of them in the craziest ways. It pleases God for us to pray for each other

I am truly blessed to have had my faith strengthened again and again. Faith allows you to drop to your knees and share all that is on your heart because you know He hears you.

Even though the Lord already knows your every thought, He Loves to see your heart at work. Secretly I think He even gets a chuckle out of the fit prayers we throw for within those we reveal passion.

God is Love in it's most unconditional form.

Faith helps with your ability to stay in today and not fret about tomorrow for you know God has always got you. You may have even taken the time to armor yourself with a bit of scripture to help you with anxiety regarding the future. This is my personal favorite reminder:

> "So do not worry about tomorrow, for tomorrow will care for itself. Each day has enough trouble of its own. (Matthew 6:34, NASB)

Anxiety is a weapon the evil one uses. If you don't believe in spiritual warfare, you should! I dress for battle every day. Even though I know my God is bigger and I have nothing to fear, I am not foolish about such things. Even Jesus tangled with the Devil. If you don't think he is a formidable foe, well, you don't truly understand how he works.

As children we all quickly learned what silent but deadly meant and when someone said that we quickly exited the room. I promise you that the evil one is as close to silent and deadly as a paid assassin. You don't see him right away and often you are already in a fight for your life before you even realize he has entered the picture.

I read a lot and I listen to great teachings on Moody Radio when I get the chance, so you will have to forgive me for I cannot recall where I first heard this but the truth in it is undeniable. Forgive me for this is not the exact quote either. I have a way of compiling information and consolidating it. With that being said, in a gist this is what I took away from the lesson; 'If you think the devil hasn't come across the likes of you, your ego is too big. He has been at this war for a couple thousand years. To date, Jesus is the only one that defeated him. Don't you think you ought to get to know Jesus?'

When I first started seeking God with all my heart and joined a bible study group, one of the first books of the bible we studied was Ephesians. That is where I learned about the armor to wear and how best to protect yourself against Satan. I would like to take you right to the book of Ephesians, beginning with Chapter 6, verse 10:

> verse 10: Finally, be strong in the Lord and in the strength of His might.

> verse 11: Put on the full armor of God, so that you will be able to stand firm against the schemes of the devil.

> verse 12: For our struggle is not against flesh and blood, but against the rulers, against the powers, against the world forces of this darkness, against the spiritual forces of wickedness in the heavenly places.

> verse 13: Therefore, take up the full armor of God, so that you will be able to resist in the evil day, and having done everything to stand firm.

> verse 14: Stand firm therefore, HAVING GIRDED YOUR LOINS WITH THE TRUTH, and HAVING PUT ON THE BREASTPLATE OF RIGHTEOUSNESS,

verse 15: and having shod YOUR FEET WITH THE PREPARATION OF THE GOSPEL OF PEACE;

verse 16: in addition to all, taking up the shield of faith with which you will be able to extinguish all the flaming arrows of the evil one.

verse 17: And take THE HELMET OF SALVATION, and the sword of the Spirit, which is the word of God. (Ephesians 6:10-17, NASB)

Quite an impressive list of armor. Today I am mainly focusing on the shield of faith and how taking it up you are able to extinguish all the flaming arrows of the evil one.

Flaming arrows, that paints quite the picture. The flaming arrows are thoughts meant to take you out. Don't fool yourself for one second. The devil is here to steal, kill and destroy. He will do that by any means possible. Including getting you to believe crazy lies. Think crazy thoughts, and do things you would not do without something, someone pushing you over the edge. These things all stem from you being bombarded with flaming arrows. Put up your shield of faith and protect yourself.

Life is a completely different scene as you learn that you truly can make a difference in this battle. All you need is Faith. Don't let the Lord say of you, "Oh ye of little faith". Stand strong in the Lord, remain firm in your belief. He came so you could live this life abundantly.

That my friends is some really good news in a world that longs to beat you down, you have a Savior. He is right here with you, waiting for you to call out so He can reveal more of His glory. It is never ending. It is a bright new day. Make the most of it!

Father I come before you today with great joy in my heart. As a child entering into the age of consent, I knew nothing about armor. I have often wondered how different my life might have turned out had I known all the truths I know today. As you tell us not to worry about tomorrow or yesterday for that matter, I know in my heart that nothing that has taken place in the past was for waste. You use all events for good. You are faithful. Your love is unconditional and I am so grateful for that. I am thankful that I recognize evil for what evil is and that I am today fully aware of my armor needed. I am so blessed to have learned about it when I did. Your timing is always perfect. I know you would have protected me through all of my recent battles regardless. In that I am confident. I also know by wearing my armor, I was able to better withstand the onslaught of attacks I faced this summer. Not only did I withstand, with your strength, I persevered. Here I am, with your help, reaching back in hopes of finding others held in the chains of bondage. Help me with this task Father. Help me be a better leader, help me to be a brighter light, help me call out to the lost and lonely, as well as the overwhelmed. Help my fellow brothers and sisters find their way home. Help them to lift their heads and see the truth. You love your children no matter what! In Jesus name I pray. Amen.

Be blessed my friends and always be a blessing to others,

Wendy Glidden, walks with God, Mom of Many

Connect with the Author

My Website: www.youareworthytoo.com

My Blog Site on Blogger:
www.youareworthytoo.blogspot.com

My Email Address: wendyglidden123@gmail.com

Like Our Ministry page on Facebook:
https://www.facebook.com/youareworthytoo

Find our page on Google!

Please spread the word

Acknowledgements

None of this would have been written without help.

Out side of The Father, the Son and the Holy Spirit, I would like to say thank you to smashwords. You made the process understandable and affordable! The education you provide all for free is a gift.

I also need to say thank you to my oldest daughter, Cassandra for reading my first book and insisting I complete this one a little quicker.

I would also like to thank my husband Mike. You have been a great support throughout this process. Thank you for being an incredible help mate. We have come a long way baby!

I could not publish this work without also thanking many of my sisters in Christ. Thank you for reading my blog posts, calling and encouraging me, as well as being there on a personal level: Joan Johns, Jean Crain, Anastashia Griffin, Tiffany Daily, Cathy Padgett, Brenda Taylor, Tracy Maynard, Amanda Anzalone, Debbie Doyle, Chalice Shannon, Nakilah Shannon, Pamela Eicher, Mardawna Grover, Kim Anders, and Elizabeth Utterback and my most recent sister in Christ, TeriLyn for reinspiring the writer in me to get back to it. Sisters in Christ. We truly do strengthen one another!

I also want to thank a couple of my brothers in Christ, Jordan Daily and Rusty Kennedy. Thank you for sharing the good news honestly and boldly. I also need to thank

Bill Cear Baugh. The one guy who continually read my blog posts and gave me a male perspective on things!

I would also like to say thank you to you, my readers. It has been the messages I have received from you that encourage me to keep writing. Paul once wrote about looking forward to being encouraged by those he intended to encourage himself. That is what the church is all about! Be blessed my friends and be a blessing to others!

Wendy Glidden

Made in the USA
Middletown, DE
29 October 2021

51244502R00141